EDUCATION IN AUSTRALIA

World Education Series

General Editors: Michael D. Stephens,
MA, MEd, PhD, FRGS

Gordon W. Roderick,
BSc, MA, PhD, MInstP
University of Liverpool

Education in
Australia

PHILLIP E. JONES
Senior Lecturer in Education,
The University of New England

DAVID & CHARLES   *Newton Abbot*
ARCHON BOOKS   *Hamden, Connecticut*
1974

For DIANA,
who has climbed the ladder . . .

This edition first published 1974 in Great Britain by
David & Charles (Holdings) Limited, Newton Abbot, Devon
and in the United States of America by Archon Books,
an imprint of The Shoe String Press, Inc, Hamden, Connecticut 06514

ISBN o 7153 6298 4 (Great Britain)
ISBN o 208-01387-3 (United States)

Set in eleven on thirteen point Imprint
and printed in Great Britain
by Latimer Trend & Company Ltd Plymouth

Contents

5

List of Figures

Foreword

To write in a balanced way about Australian education is no easy task. He who tries may well be accused of bias, of ignoring features of educational development in some parts of Australia, or of unduly emphasising features in a certain state or of a particular section of education. In this book, the author has attempted to show the development of Australian education in the light of generally held political values and of the country's political structure. If there appears to be an emphasis on New South Wales, it is because that state has had an important influence on others, both historically and in terms of innovatory practices. Inevitably, it is difficult to select, from among six states, those developments which are the most interesting; rather the attempt has been made to select particularly significant and illustrative ones.

The writer's assessment has been made at a time which may well be a watershed for educational development in Australia. The role of the Commonwealth government and a change in political outlook, as a result of the Labor Party victory in the 1972 Federal elections, have therefore been emphasised, so far as it is possible to do so in the space of a short work such as this.

I

Equality and Aspiration

QUITE early in his school life the Australian child learns that his country is both the world's smallest continent and its largest island. Traditionally he has been conditioned to Australia's British heritage, but today he not only learns that his country is bounded by the vast expanses of the Indian Ocean on the west and the Pacific on the east, but also that his country lies to the south of many tropical developing nations—Malaysia, the Philippines, Indonesia, New Guinea. A little to the east lies New Zealand, but beyond that are thousands of small islands in a vast ocean. His is an isolated land. The tropic of Capricorn passes through the northern parts of Australia, and also through South America and Africa, but of these distant continents he knows little.

With an area of almost three million square miles Australia is approximately the size of the USA. Australia has huge inland areas which are largely desert and, except for nomadic aborigines and white managers and stockmen of cattle stations, are almost uninhabited. It is the world's most sparsely populated continent, having a density of about only four persons per square mile, for the supply of water is, and always has been, Australia's main problem. Forty per cent of the country receives less than 10 inches of rain each year, while only about 10 per cent receives more than 40 inches—almost entirely concentrated on the north Queensland coast, a distinctly tropical area. The combination of high temperatures and erratic rainfall results in frequent droughts; indeed, much of the efficiency of precipitation is lost through high evaporation rates. Yet because of the country's

9

size remarkable extremes of climatic conditions occur, including a pleasant, temperate climate in more southerly coastal regions, and snow and low temperatures in the Australian Alps and in parts of Tasmania, the Australian island state lying to the south of Victoria.

Mountains are the exception rather than the norm in Australia. A minority of the land mass is higher than 1,000 feet above sea level; the main exception to the general flatness, especially of the inland landscape, is the Great Dividing Range which parallels the eastern coastline and serves to squeeze most of the population into narrow coastal areas. At the same time, a few tableland areas or mountain ranges are found in the north and north-west of the continent, and in South Australia. As a result there is a dearth of major river systems, no large reliable streams being found from the Murray-Darling river system in western New South Wales to the Indian Ocean. Inland, therefore, it is often necessary to rely on artesian bores for water, particularly for stock. East of the Great Divide, a number of short swift rivers are to be found and their existence is reflected in the settlement pattern and population density.

Consequently, Australia has an unusual population distribution. More than 80 per cent of the nation's people are concentrated in the south-eastern corner of the well-watered states of Victoria and New South Wales. Eight of every ten of these people live in urban areas and more than 50 per cent of the total Australian population of 13 millions live in the capital cities. Melbourne, for example, contains 65 per cent of Victoria's population. Sydney and Melbourne combined contain about 40 per cent of the nation's people.

The stereotype of Australia presented to the outside world is of 'the bush' or 'outback'; the reality is urban centres, and more particularly the domination of state capital cities, to which all eyes, including those of farmers and graziers in the drier parts, turn.

The capital cities are significant in another sense as well. The Australian schoolchild also learns at an early age that Australia is divided into six states, each with a seaboard capital city and a parliament of its own, and that the states have been federated (since 1901) in the Commonwealth of Australia, with head-quarters at Canberra in the Australian Capital Territory, about midway between Australia's two largest cities—Sydney, capital of New South Wales, and Melbourne, capital of Victoria. The largest state is Western Australia (Perth is the capital), and the most populous and oldest, New South Wales. The Federal government is responsible for defence, foreign affairs, customs, pensions, the collection of income tax, postal services, certain territories (including the Northern Territory which covers Darwin and the 'dead heart' around Alice Springs in the centre of the continent) and other functions delegated to it by the constitution, but not education, mines, hospitals, most land transport, and certain other functions traditionally reserved to the states.

A NEW COUNTRY—A NEW OPPORTUNITY

Discovery and settlement   Australia is, geologically speaking, an old country, yet it is new by discovery. Three hundred years ago, the western world did not know for certain whether the Great South Land existed or not. During the seventeenth century ships of the Dutch East Indies fleets touched on and explored parts of the northern and western coasts, while in 1642 Abel Tasman discovered part of Tasmania which he named Van Diemen's Land. An Englishman, William Dampier, also visited the coast of western Australia in 1688 and 1699 but, like the Dutch, he was not greatly impressed either by the aboriginal inhabitants or by the possibilities the land held for trade.

Almost another hundred years passed before Captain James Cook's exploration of New Zealand and his discovery of the east coast of the South Land in 1770. Cook claimed the whole of the eastern part of New Holland (as the land was then generally known) for the British Crown and called it New South Wales (see map on p 13). Following the loss of the North American colonies, the

British government in time sought a new location for felons from
its overflowing prisons and Botany Bay, where Cook had landed
on the east coast, was chosen as a convict settlement. Thus,
eighteen years after Cook's visit, the first British settlement in
New Holland was established with the arrival of Captain Arthur
Phillip and his fleet in 1788. Phillip determined not to settle at
Botany Bay, but in nearby Port Jackson, which he declared was
'the finest harbour in the world', had better soil than sandy
Botany Bay and provided reasonable supplies of fresh water.
Sydney was to be the beginning of a set of vigorous colonies,
although the gaol and military atmosphere, and the extreme
difficulties of that first settlement, hardly augured well for the
future.

Within a few years of the arrival of the 'first fleet', the exploration of inland Australia began. The Blue Mountains, a forbidding
part of the Great Dividing Range barring the way west about
thirty-five miles from Sydney, were crossed in 1813 and this
achievement was quickly followed by epic journeys of exploration
to the north, south and west. Among these were the explorations
of John Oxley, Surveyor-General; Hume and Hovell in 1824 to
Westernport, near the later site of Melbourne; Cunningham to
the north as far as the Darling Downs and the convict settlement
at Moreton Bay (Brisbane in Queensland), and Captain Charles
Sturt who, by tracing the Darling and Murray rivers to their
mouth in what is now South Australia, dispelled an early colonial
myth that an inland sea existed in the interior of the continent.
Many were the epics of inland exploration.

Meanwhile, British settlements had been made in Van
Diemen's Land in 1803, Moreton Bay in 1824, King George's
Sound (Western Australia) in 1826 and at Portland Bay (now
part of Victoria) in 1834. Adelaide, the capital of a new colony
of South Australia, was settled in 1836, and was something of a
change in British settlement, for no convicts were involved. Indeed, by this time the era of transportation was almost at an end
in the eastern colonies and free settlers were arriving in increasing

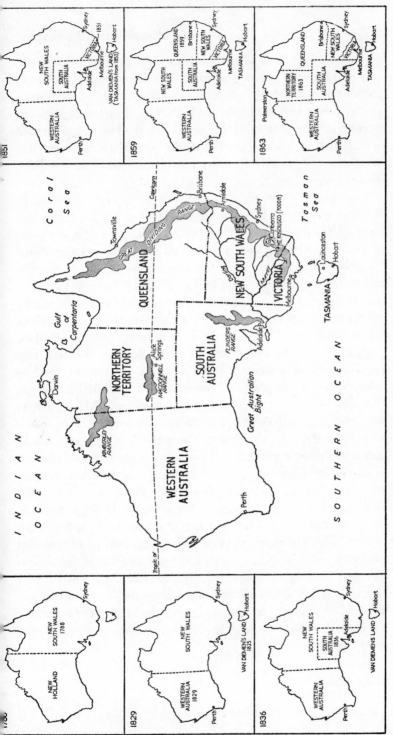

Fig 1 Map of Australia, showing the establishment of separate Australian colonies

numbers. The worth of many inland areas for pastoral use was now more readily appreciated and the frontier was subsequently pushed further back by the explorations of Leichhardt and others, and by Burke and Wills who made the first crossing of the continent from south to north in 1860–1. By the late 1860s it could be said that a good proportion of the Australian continent had been explored, largely by British subjects. Gold had also been discovered.

The nature of the early colonial settlements is important. In the first place they laid the foundations for a more religiously heterogeneous population than in the motherland. The convicts, including many from Ireland, were a mixed group who had been sentenced to transportation for between seven years and life and who came from all walks of life. The Irish brought Catholicism with them and a strong association grew between Catholic priests and lower classes in the original colony. This, and subsequent Protestant alarm, laid the basis for early sectarian clashes, particularly on the education question. Second, the relatively rapid spread of settlement was caused in part by the need to found more severe places of punishment for recalcitrant felons (Norfolk Island, Newcastle, Port Macquarie and Moreton Bay, for example), and in part by the fear of settlement by other powers, in particular the French who at the time were particularly active in Pacific exploration. Tasmanian settlement was partly a reaction to this, as was the first attempt to settle Western Australia in 1826. In the third place, many convicts were granted their freedom and, although without means, began a new life as free settlers. Freedom and better opportunity under harsh sun and blue sky appealed more than the tyranny and repression of the old world! As the years passed, the number of free immigrants from England increased; by this time the possibilities of the inland for sheep raising were becoming apparent and a pastoral community developed, largely as the result of squatting on extensive tracts of land beyond the effective control of seaboard government.

Early education and the religious question   Until the middle of the nineteenth century, educational provision in the Australian colonies was generally haphazard. With the exception of a few fee-paying, grammar-type, church-sponsored schools for the children of an emerging more well-to-do colonial élite, schooling was, for the most part, provided in primitive conditions and by untrained men and women, frequently ex-convicts. Sectarian rivalries and disputes about the respective roles of church and state in the control of education prevented the early establishment of a uniform and satisfactory education system, and the spread of settlement over vast distances made any comprehensive provision difficult.

Indeed, in New South Wales and Tasmania the early governors, though aware of—and concerned about—the problem of providing schooling for the growing number of school-age colonial children, were necessarily preoccupied with other difficulties of settlement in a large, dry and often inhospitable land. In tune with what was happening in England, the churches, and especially the Church of England, saw themselves as the proper agents of education. By themselves they did not have the necessary financial resources and, like others in the colonies, turned to the state for help. At first, the British government did not accept the principle of financial support for education, but the colonial governors did, and attempted to obtain finance through local tax measures. Consequently there was early recognition of the need for government aid for education, which supplemented the small financial grants of missionary organisations such as the Society for the Propagation of the Gospel and the London Missionary Society.

In 1826 the Church and Schools Corporation was established. At the inspiration of the Church of England authorities in England and the Colonial Office, one-seventh of the land in each county of New South Wales was to be set aside 'for the maintainance of the Church and the education of the youth in New South Wales'.[1] The privileged position which was thus conferred upon the Anglican Church (in times of Catholic emancipation in the motherland) intensified sectarian bitterness which forced the demise of the corporation by 1833. As an alternative to an Anglican-dominated school system, Governor Bourke attempted to introduce the Irish National System into the colony. This scheme provided for the establishment of government non-denominational schools 'to bring together children from all sects for a general literary education'.[2] Strong opposition from quarters other than Roman Catholic, largely because of the scheme's label as 'Irish', forced the abandonment of the proposal. In its stead the government introduced a pound for pound subsidy, called the 'half and half' system, for denominational schools.

Sectarian rivalries likewise precluded the introduction, by Governor Gipps in 1840, of an educational system modelled on the British and Foreign School Society. The proposal to exclude denominational religious teaching, but allow the free use of the Bible in schools, failed to win Protestant support. In 1844 a Select Committee of the New South Wales Legislative Council, chaired by Robert Lowe, investigated educational provision and again recommended the implementation of the Irish National System. Aware that clerical opposition remained uncompromising on the education issue and preoccupied with other problems (for example, the land question), Gipps did not introduce the system.

However, times and circumstances were changing. A 'dual' education system of church and state schools, in part essentially similar to the Irish National System, was established by Governor Fitzroy in 1848. Under this arrangement, government aid for schools was given to the various denominations through a Board of Denominational Education, while a Board of National Education was responsible, and given financial backing, for the commencement of a system of state-controlled, non-denominational, or 'National' schools. The latter board proved to be extremely vigorous. Agents travelled throughout the colony encouraging and organising the establishment of national schools and by 1851 twenty-two such schools were in operation, with a further nineteen awaiting approval and finance. Local support for building schoolhouses was strong, but the National Board had a massive problem in finding suitable teachers: some were immigrants, but an effort to train local inhabitants at a model school in Sydney was reasonably successful. William Wilkins, appointed headmaster of the school and later a board inspector, together with Henry Parkes, also an immigrant and partisan of state education, were influential in furthering the campaign for a unified educational system. In 1866 the New South Wales Public Schools Act abolished the two boards and created a Council of Education with control both over 'public' (previously 'national') schools, whose numbers grew very rapidly from this point onwards, and also over denominational schools, whose operation henceforth was hedged with restrictions and the numbers of which started to decline. The sectarian question in education was steadily being resolved in favour of a government, non-denominational school system.

Educational problems and provision in the other colonies bore a strong resemblance to those in New South Wales. In Van Diemen's Land (Tasmania) and Western Australia sectarian rivalries prevented the establishment of a unified educational system for many years. In South Australia government interference in education was strongly opposed, so much so that government grants, commenced in 1846, were withdrawn from the denominations in 1851. In this latter year Victoria was established as a separate colony, with Queensland carved off from New South Wales in 1859. In both of the new colonies, legislation was eventually passed withdrawing grants for denominational schools and firmly establishing public educational systems.

Pastoral expansion, gold and immigration Undoubtedly, the two most important factors in the making of Australia in the first sixty years of the nineteenth century were the development of rural industry and the discovery of gold. Despite the attempts of the authorities to limit the area of settlement, settlers in New South Wales, bent on pastoral pursuits, ignored them and went

B

beyond the nineteen counties (officially the limit of settlement in 1829). Moreover, development in Victoria, with its rich pastures, was also rapid. Melbourne had been settled in 1836. R. M. Crawford remarks:

> In 1840, after a mere four years of settlement, Melbourne's population exceeded 10,000 and there were 800,000 sheep. By 1847, with the depression in between, there were close on 43,000 people and over 4,000,000 sheep. Four years later, on the eve of the Gold Rushes, there were 77,000 people in the colony of Victoria, with 6,000,000 sheep and close on 400,000 head of cattle on its pastures.[3]

In outback areas, pursuit of the pastoral life was very lonely. On reflection, many Australian writers agree that a strong feeling of group solidarity and loyalty developed out of the sense of isolation in the bush. It has been suggested that the almost complete absence of religious facilities in the outback resulted in the reinforcement of the bush workers' 'already strong feeling of mateship, and their propensity to mutual aid'.[4] This is reflected in Australian literature, particularly that of the closing years of the nineteenth century.

The second factor of immense importance was the discovery of gold in 1851. In the ten years which followed, Australia's population almost trebled, but not many of the diggers struck riches. Nevertheless, many of them stayed, either on the land or in commercial enterprises in the seaboard capitals. According to Russel Ward:

> Mateship, and that curiously unconventional yet powerful collectivist morality, were two important elements of the pastoral workers' ethos which were taken over by the diggers. It is true that life on the fields lacked the loneliness of station work, but on the other hand, alluvial mining could be performed effectively only by teams of at least two or three men. On some 'wet' claims, as many as ten to fourteen men had to work together. . . . The fact that members of these teams were universally known as 'mates' suggests the influence of the pre-existing tradition.[5]

Thus it appears that one important effect of the gold rushes was

to increase the Australian trait of 'mateship'. Another effect was
the new attitudes of the immigrants who sought for better social
conditions than they had enjoyed in the country of their birth.
These included a call for education.

The impetus to educational development from about 1860
onwards was occasioned not only by native-born Australians;
immigrants also played a major role. For newly landed arrivals in
a strange new country there was an exciting sense of starting anew,
free from the evils of the old world. Radical democrats in the
antipodes thought of freedom, not merely in the political sense,
but also as equality for all to enjoy the benefits of a new, less
class-stratified society. This included education, and for both
the town youngster and the isolated rural child. So strong has
this egalitarian sentiment grown, that it may still be distinguished
in policies relating to education.

In New South Wales, after the establishment of the Council of
Education in 1866, it was necessary to have a guaranteed attendance of twenty-five school pupils before a public school could be
opened. What were, for many years, subsequently known as
'provisional' schools were set up where the minimum number
was somewhat less; in addition, 'half-time' schools, staffed by
itinerant teachers, were also established and, for a time, provided
reasonably for rural needs. Some idea of the improvements in
education in the Australian outback may be gained from the
increase in these schools and in the numbers attending them.
Between 1867 and 1877 the number of provisional schools increased from 31 to 266, and attendance from 476 to 5,324. Half-
time schools rose from 6 to 112 and the enrolments proportion-
ately.[6] At the same time, facilities were being extended steadily
in urban areas, so that, under the auspices of the colonial government, a non-sectarian form of primary education was provided
for an increasing proportion of colonial youth. As yet, most
secondary education, where provided, was private in nature and
only for the children of a colonial social élite, while Sydney University, established at mid-century, had few enrolments.

Free, compulsory and secular schooling? Although a period of alternating boom and depression, the last thirty years of the nineteenth century were decades of remarkable development in Australia. The wild colonial boys and bushranging gave way to astute politicians and emerging nationhood. With increased population the towns grew, commercial enterprise thrived on the pastoral and increasingly varied agricultural industries, and on meeting the needs of a larger population; railways and roads put a permanent touch to the bullock tracks between coastal port and inland sheep station. Wheat became an industry of great importance, a trade union movement—an organised form of mateship—emerged, and a Federation movement grew apace. Rough though many aspects of life may still have been, the six colonies were moving towards maturity.

Not the least important of the trends of the time was the development of education. And it was in this period, too, that events were to shape the form of the present-day educational organisation and administration characteristic of mid-twentieth-century Australia. Between 1872 and 1893 all six colonies passed legislation which established government-controlled school systems under a Minister of the Crown and withdrew financial aid to church schools; these statutes were popularly known as the 'free, compulsory and secular' Acts, although not in every instance did they entirely succeed in attaining these objectives in practice.[7] Nevertheless, they did succeed in solving, for a long time, the religious question. In New South Wales, for instance, under the Council of Education (from 1866) church schools were allowed to continue and received financial assistance, but under severe restrictions which favoured the government schools. Following the passage of the 1880 Public Instruction Act in that colony, 'state aid' to church schools was withdrawn as from the end of 1882, and colonial funds for education were henceforth directed to public schools. Nevertheless this legislation did not immediately make education at public schools free (threepence a week remained a charge for some years), nor did it make attendance compulsory (despite truant officers and court cases) until amending legislation in 1916. And the Act certainly did not result in a fully secular education, since clergy entry to public schools to give denominational religious instruction continued to be permitted, and the primary course of study required regular teachers to give Bible lessons from specially prepared readers. Children could also leave school before the end of the compulsory school attendance period if they showed evidence of reaching the required academic standard.

What happened to the church schools? Religious authorities were divided on the issue of government aid; most Protestant schools closed, or had already done so, while many Anglican schools without strong financial backing (usually those established by parishes) likewise shut their doors. Anglicans themselves were divided on the question of the church role in education, just as they were, and still are, on aspects of doctrine. In the event, only a few Anglican schools survived. Some closed in later decades, but a handful, catering for a social élite, expanded and thrived. It was the Roman Catholic authorities who, believing that government schools were 'seed beds of vice', refused to let the withdrawal of aid stop their educational efforts. They resolved to hold on to—and, indeed, expand—their own religious school system, unaided by the state. By raising money from their congregations to build and equip more schools and by recruiting religious teaching orders from overseas to administer and staff them, they succeeded in their objective, although undoubtedly not without much sacrifice and, in all probability, some coercion of the faithful. Thus was established the pattern of a dual system of government and non-government schools which has persisted to the present day.

The early grammar-type secondary schools of colonial Australia aimed at the production of the 'educated Christian gentleman'. Towards the end of the nineteenth century they were joined by state secondary schools, few in number and often poorly supported, but offering the talented youngster—boy and girl—of ambitious working- or middle-class parents an imitation on a day basis of the kind of intellectual education provided for the more fortunate upper sections of colonial society.[8] In New South Wales, for example, following the passage of the 1880 Public Instruction Act, eight high schools were opened, but by the turn of the century only four of them had survived. Part of the reason for their unpopularity was the existence of 'superior public' schools providing elementary education together with some senior classes, at far less cost than the few guineas per term charged by the new high schools. Further, officers of the new colonial departments of public instruction also failed to promote secondary education, as their attention was firmly fixed on what they saw as their main task, the stimulation of literacy.

It is a useful generalisation that the principal concern of the emerging colonial education bureaucracies in the late nineteenth century was to spread primary education as far and as wide as possible. As has been stressed, this was a period of considerable economic and commercial growth, and it also saw the beginnings of industrialisation and of intensifying urbanisation. These trends meant that workers must increasingly be literate. In addition, however, the sentiment was by now common in Australia that all children should have an education; the opportunity for it must be offered, and provided by 'the government'. What the officers of colonial departments of public instruction understood, and what politicians understood the public wanted, was a primary education; hence, by the turn of the century, under public auspices, schooling for children to the age of about twelve years was provided in both town and country.

A NEW CENTURY—NEW ASPIRATIONS

Secondary education for the talented or for all?   It is also a useful generalisation that the first half of the twentieth century was a period of secondary education development. It was one of the first tasks of educational administrators of the present century to put formal public secondary education on an organised basis, with a direct link with primary education and also with university entrance. In New South Wales this was arranged in the years between 1909 and 1913;[9] thereafter, state high schools began to proliferate, and help by way of bursaries for poorer children was provided, indicative of the fact that the population now desired a greater degree of public education at secondary level and that the community needed this extension of educational opportunity. It is interesting to note that, in the case of New South Wales, entry to such classes was competitive, and courses were graded on an ability basis in content, length and award. By the 1920s, however, moves were afoot to provide a common secondary course for all children who wished to continue their education. Indeed, in the period between the wars (1919–39), Australian educational thought was influenced not a little by the call in 'the old country' for 'secondary education for all' and by the dawning knowledge that in the United States secondary education for all was not merely an accepted concept, but already advanced in practice. Increasingly, progress towards the goal of universal secondary education was accepted as desirable by educational authorities in Australia, but the necessary funds to achieve this equality provided a constant difficulty and brake on the movement.

What the state had achieved was, first, education for an élite of talent (not merely a social élite) and, second, an acceptance of a desire for general educational upgrading in the community generally. It was, however, not until after World War II that publicly provided secondary education was seen more fully as the education of all adolescents and that the academic bias of the secondary school, which clearly existed between the wars, was broken.

Australia appears to have experienced certain periods of social conscience in its history: one of these was just after the federation of the six colonies in the Commonwealth of Australia in 1901. The new Federal, or Commonwealth, government embarked on a programme of social legislation which included a people's bank,

old age pensions and similar measures. Thus, in the first decade
or so of the new century social changes of considerable moment
resulted from an air of optimism (a sense of national fulfilment
making possible the achievement of social objectives) and the
rise to power of the Labor Party which developed from embryonic
trade union organisation in the eighties and nineties and was
fully committed to changing the older order. It was in this
atmosphere of social conscience, then, that state systems of
secondary education were established.

During the twenties another wave of immigration strained the
resources of primary schools to the limit and, in some conservative quarters, there was a reluctance to provide more secondary
education if it meant the neglect of basic education for all.
However, the growth of the apprenticeship system, following
further industrialisation during World War I, accentuated the
need for at least junior secondary education. In addition, several
experiments in the organisation of secondary schools took place,
among them the area schools of Tasmania in the thirties.

Disruption by depression and war   What progress could
be made, however, was dealt a severe blow by the depression of
the 1930s which hit the schools of all states very hard. One result
of tragic economic times was a growth in secondary school enrolments, since young people, like their elders, just could not find
work. At the same time, teachers' salaries were cut in the interests of economy, and the recruitment of trainee teachers into
teachers' colleges was severely pruned. Indeed, in one or two
instances these colleges closed their doors. By the time World
War II broke out in September 1939, the schools and colleges
had by no means recovered from the effects of depression, and
they were to be affected almost as severely by wartime restrictions. Thus the thirties and early forties were not propitious
times for educational development in Australia.

Perhaps it was the cataclysmic economic and political events
of the time which almost made education a non-issue, about
which—in contrast to the reform conscience of a few decades

earlier—there seemed to be little thought or concern. Yet, despite this, there was progress: for example, in 1937 a series of conferences across Australia resulted in the formation of a New Education Fellowship, and the ideas aired on these occasions brought a fresh breeze, if not a gale, of educational discussion. At about the same time an Australian Council for Educational Research was formed (more will be said about the work of this organisation in later chapters). There was also some much needed experimentation in school architecture, but of course funds were limited for updating on a grand scale. One most interesting development was the commencement of 'opportunity classes' for intellectually gifted children in Sydney in 1932, again on a small scale, but the harbinger of developments to come.

During this rather quiet period in Australian educational development, two very important things had been taking place. First, the colonial bureaucracies of education officials and inspectors of schools had been consolidated after reorganisation in the early years of the century. Patterns of centralised administration proved to be remarkably similar from state to state and their rigidity would be difficult to break, or even modify. Second, there had been at least one major reform from inside the systems, with help from overseas educational ideas, and this was the development of kindergarten classes. Influenced by ideas like those of Froebel and Montessori, infants' grade teachers remade the curriculum and utilised methods of teaching much more suitable for five- to eight-year-old children, so that by the end of the thirties it could at least be said that the first two or three years of school life were in keeping with the latest ideas of educational philosophers and psychologists. For the very young, the regimentation and unhappiness of the nineteenth-century schoolroom had largely passed.

It was not, therefore, unexpected that similar changes would occur in other classrooms, but these had to await the cessation of hostilities in 1945 and the return to normality. Still, some progress was made, even in wartime. For example, one of the highly constraining factors on curriculum and methods in primary schools in New South Wales had for years been the existence, at the conclusion of primary school, of an external examination for selection for entry to various types of secondary school. Just before and during the war period, this examination hurdle was first modified and then phased out. It was replaced by an assessment of intellectual and academic ability not requiring a formal test. This was to be a highly significant change, influencing not only the atmosphere of the primary grades, but also the form and function of the secondary school as well.

More important still, however, was the changed kind of community emerging from a conflict which had come so close to Australia's shores. There was prosperity, full employment, and hope for a better future. A new generation of parents, whose own education had been during depression and war, aspired to better things for their children. In a now even more industrialised and urbanised post-war Australia, most of them saw a good education as a necessity for their offspring, and were determined to get it for them.

University development   Until World War II university development in Australia was slow. Established by colonial (later state) governments, and largely financed by them, the universities had not been seen as playing a major role in national development prior to 1939, and the topic appropriately finds its place in this chapter as a postscript. The first university, Sydney, was established in 1850, but its early years saw a preoccupation with classical, liberal education; by 1880 only seventy-six students were enrolled. Its offerings were largely out of touch with the practical needs and the pragmatic temper of colonial society. However, extensions to courses and internal reforms took place shortly afterwards (for example, faculties of science and medicine were established, women became eligible for enrolment, and part-time evening classes were introduced). By 1909 enrolment stood at some 1,300.

It was following the reorganisation of secondary education in

New South Wales in the years around 1912 that university growth reflected the impact of a growing middle professional group in Australian society. The number of bequests increased and it was possible to expand the curriculum with faculties of engineering, dentistry, veterinary science, agriculture, architecture, and so on. The expansion of the 1920s was followed by rural developments like Canberra University College (under the control of the University of Melbourne) in 1930, and the New England University College at Armidale (under the University of Sydney) in 1938. Much earlier, of course, a state university had been established in each of the other five states: Melbourne in 1853 and the last, Western Australia, in 1911. Their development was likewise slow, but steady; Melbourne became a large institution like Sydney, and the University of Western Australia attracted attention for its policy of free tuition to those admitted as undergraduates. The expansion of tertiary education, a clear reflection of growing aspirations, was to be a feature of the third quarter of the century.

This chapter has endeavoured to show how the themes of equality, opportunity and rising aspiration in Australia largely directed the development of education systems up to 1945. While for the most part educational ideas came from overseas, the people who used them applied their own expectations, their own form of government and the social opportunity of a more egalitarian society to mould them to their own situation. This, however, was destined to develop and change even more in the next quarter-century.

2

The Education Explosion

WITHOUT a doubt, the educational historian of 200 years hence will find educational development between about 1945 and the present time a complex, crowded and interesting subject. He will find abundant material with which to devise theories explaining why expansion and change have occurred with such rapidity not only in Australia but in other countries as well. He may well typify the events of the period, as some contemporary observers have, in terms of explosions of knowledge, population and aspirations during a time of rapid social change never before experienced in man's history. This chapter takes up the theme of the rapidity of change, as it concerns education in Australia, and also pursues a theme of the previous chapter, namely rising community aspirations for more and better education. It attempts to set these matters against the kind of educational organisation and administration which emerged during the period prior to 1945, and which has been consolidated in the post-war period.

DECADES OF EXPANSION AND CHANGE, 1950–70

Some idea of the growth of education in Australia in the period 1950–70 can be given by overall numerical tallies and also by percentage increases.[1] (See also tables on pp 37–9.) Schools, for example, showed a rise in number from 9,680 in 1950 to 10,095 in 1960, but thereafter a drop to below the 1950 figure, namely 9,650 in 1970, a reflection of the trend towards consolidation of schools (that is, the closure of many one-teacher rural schools and the growth of subsidised bus services for the conveyance of children to larger schools). On the other hand, the number of students attending school in Australia rose by about 57 per cent in the period 1950–60, to more than 2,100,000; the figure had increased to 2,768,233 in 1970, a further 30 per cent rise on 1960 statistics. Put another way, the number of school students had doubled during the twenty-year period. Despite claims that there is a teacher shortage in Australia in proportions amounting to crisis, the number of teachers in service has grown at a greater rate than the number of pupils: from just under 50,000 teachers in 1950, the figure grew to more than 74,000 (a rise of about 50 per cent) by 1960, and to 120,000 (a rise of another 60 per cent) by 1970. Shortages doubtless persist, but the pupil/teacher ratio is inevitably improved, and more specialist teachers are available.

Even greater rises have taken place in tertiary education over the same time. The number of universities has grown from 9 to 15 (and will rise further during the seventies) while enrolments have increased from about 30,000 in 1950 to almost 117,000 in 1970, over three times as many. The 1972 figure shows that the university population continues to expand (to about 128,000) but at a slightly lower rate. Doubtless this can be explained by the creation and expansion of colleges of advanced education whose enrolments have been increasing by about 20 per cent a year, to 44,500 in 1971. Figures for the following year show that the total enrolled is divided approximately equally between full-time students, and part-time and external students, and that almost one-half of the total is enrolled in colleges of advanced education in the state of Victoria. Most of the students are enrolled in commercial and business studies, and the next most important group are those taking engineering and technical courses.

A lesser known and appreciated feature of educational expansion has been the growth in the number of technical colleges and their enrolments. From 141 technical colleges in 1950, the number grew to 296 in 1969; this means that facilities in terms of the number of colleges doubled during the period, but the number of students attending increased from 161,500 to just over 398,000 in 1969, a considerably greater rise. Although teachers' colleges did not increase by anything like the same number—rather, existing colleges tended to become much larger, or to cater for more students in overcrowded conditions—the numbers of students in training rose sharply, as might be guessed from the improved teacher supply relative to increased school enrolments. A particularly welcome rise in teacher trainees occurred in the period 1968–70 when enrolments rose by 36 per cent.

Immigration   An important social phenomenon affecting Australian life since World War II has been the immigration programme. Both in the nineteenth century (during the Gold Rushes) and in the twenties (British immigration) there were social changes of magnitude arising from migration, but the more cosmopolitan nature of a huge influx of newcomers since 1945 has yet to be fully assessed. By 1947 Australia's population was approximately 7·5 million. The Federal government had initiated a programme for receiving displaced persons from war-torn Europe. This grew into a massive immigration programme that added some 2·5 million people in just over twenty-five years (total Australian population by 1972 was estimated at 13 million). Of the arguments used to support immigration (and politically there were few voices raised against the policy) probably the most cogent was that of 'populate or perish'; in addition, the migrant intake assisted the provision of low-skilled workers for expanding secondary industry.

A considerable amount of Federal funding has sustained the programme. In addition to assisted passages for many settlers temporary hostel and housing accommodation has had to be provided, English language classes established and maintained, and additional school accommodation built. In terms of sheer numbers the programme has meant much to Australia, as has the changing, more cosmopolitan nature of community customs, and the variety of influences people of different countries have had on Australian mores and attitudes. Until relatively recently, however, native-born Australians have tended to take immigration for granted and have conveniently ignored the problems large-scale migration poses.

One such problem is the education of migrant children. Early in the 1970s the Commonwealth government reacted to the small, but growing, amount of evidence of unsatisfactory adjustment by many non-English migrants by providing added assistance for English classes.[2] At school level, however, little has been done towards training teachers specifically to assist in teaching migrant children, a problem in urban areas where national groups, rather naturally, tend to congregate together. Overall, very little has been spent on meeting the educational problems of immigrants and there is, in addition, some evidence that migration has caused a rise in juvenile delinquency, although at the same time stories of migrant children 'making good' are to be found in almost every school.

All told, migrants have come from about sixty countries: approximately 45 per cent are from Great Britain and about 40 per cent from Europe. The number of assisted migrants in 1964, for instance, was nearly 80,000 and in 1970 it had risen to a peak of 134,000.[3] In the first nine months of 1971, of 115,000 arrivals, 43,000 came from Great Britain (including Ireland), 8,600 from Yugoslavia and 9,400 from Italy, 6,400 from Greece and 5,700 from Austria.[4] Perhaps surprisingly, 5,000 arrived from the United States and just over 3,000 from Germany. In view of the huge numbers involved, really very few leave Australia to return home. For most of the period jobs have been plentiful and there is probably less prejudice by Australians against newcomers than was, perhaps, the case a quarter of a century ago. Nevertheless, there is some disquiet about migrant ghettos, and about the fact that, in economically difficult times, it is an unskilled migrant worker who loses his job first.

Migration has combined with a high rate of natural increase in the Australian population to intensify the population explosion which has occurred to much the same extent elsewhere in the world during recent decades. Indeed, after the conclusion of World War II, the explosions of population, knowledge and aspirations (to which many social scientists continually make pertinent reference) had marked effects on Australian education. There is no doubt that immigration and high fertility rates have made for severe logistic problems facing Australian departments of education and independent schools. While evidence for immigrant aspirations is hard to quantify, aspiration for a better life —just as in the case of earlier migrant groups—is definitely present. The native-born Australian child is also pressured by his parents to achieve more than they did. Of the knowledge explosion, little need be said: its effect is self-evident in the increasingly complex, technological and urbanised Australian society. At the time of writing, some doubts are being expressed about immigration, but hardly on the basis of much objective evidence; some politicians are calling for the abandonment of all assisted immigration, others for a more selective policy. It has been claimed that Australia's rapidly growing population has in fact inhibited the rate of economic growth, and has been prejudicial to material living standards.[5] With a 30 per cent cut in assisted immigration by Australia's new Labor government at the end of 1972, clearly a period of reassessment of the immigration policy is at hand.

Promoting human welfare   The rise in the number of students at school and college, together with the effect of a large migrant increase, suggests the obvious theme affecting Australian education over more than two decades. It has been possible to cater for these changes in an increasingly affluent society, riding through a period of economic boom on the sheep's back. For although now highly industrialised, Australia still depends to some extent on the wealth which comes from the land. With the drop in world wool prices in the late sixties, however, more uncertain economic times replaced the years of boom and, with

continuing inflation, finding more and more funds for educational
purposes has become increasingly difficult. Yet, throughout the
period under review, there have been many who argue that, even
in the best of times, little enough has been spent on Australian
educational services.

Summing up the situation in 1964, R. W. T. Cowan pointed
to the rapid growth of public interest in education which he felt
had been caused by two main factors: 'the acceptance by Australians in general of the doctrine that, both nationally and inter-
nationally, the future belongs to the best educated', and 'the
awakening of many individuals to the fact that current Australian
educational resources are incapable of carrying out satisfactorily
the task of educating and training their children'. According to
Cowan, these two factors had political implications in that
governments became aware of community interest and concern,
and reacted accordingly.[6] There has been much criticism and
suggestion; it is not true to say that little has been done. There
have been changes, but whether or not they have been really
fundamental ones is problematical.

Yet educational expansion and change have been important.
As early as 1956 the Australian Council for Educational Research
indicated the trends that it saw affecting Australian education.
It emphasised the already increasing participation of the Commonwealth government in educational matters, especially the
universities; a successful attempt 'by providing bursaries and
scholarships, to encourage children to stay at school to complete
a full secondary course and . . . to continue their studies at the
tertiary level'; and 'greater attention . . . to the handicapped and
maladjusted . . . symptomatic of a steadily deepening concern
with the individual child in the school.' A fourth point made by
the council was the thought being given to questions of teacher
training; fifth, 'a pronounced movement away from supervision
and assessment of teachers by inspectors, towards assistance and
enlightenment'; and, sixth, the enhanced status of technical and
technological education.[7] The interesting thing is that emphasis

C

on these trends continued after 1956, and there is *still* concern
about them—indeed, far more concern than public discussion
admitted in 1956. Basically, as P. R. Cole wrote as early as 1937,

> The aim of education, as it is understood in Australia and else-
> where, is human welfare—health, ability to earn a living and to
> serve the common good, social qualities, taste and sentiment,
> knowledge, character and the right use of leisure. These essen-
> tials, which every teacher ought to hold in mind, are equally the
> heritage of the rural and of the urban child.[8]

And it is undoubtedly the concern for human welfare both of
the city and country child which has guided the more recent
expansion and change, to a degree unparalleled in Australian
education.

EXPANSION OF EDUCATIONAL SERVICES

The Australian Commonwealth government established a Commonwealth Office of Education in 1946; this move signalled
increasing Federal commitment to such special educational
problems as the training of ex-servicemen and women. The
official journal of the new office, *Education News*, gave an interesting review of educational development in Australia at the
time of the Commonwealth's Jubilee in 1951. Professor G. S.
Browne of the University of Melbourne presented therein a list
of features which he considered were characteristic of state educational development since federation. These included the similarity of educational development in the six states; the centralised
and authoritarian control (with little teacher freedom) in each;
freedom from church control in the public, or state, schools; the
lack of local participation in school affairs (despite the existence
of parent organisations); the continuance of sound work in 'the
fundamentals' in the schools; the existence of good educational
facilities in rural districts; the fairly strict control of teachers by
inspectors through rigid and 'daunting' promotion systems, and
the existence of a high degree of 'in-breeding' through the recruitment of inspectors and administrators from within each service.

Browne stressed the extent to which this practice led to conformity rather than providing variety.[9] Has subsequent expansion changed all these characteristics? It is doubtful.

Effects of increased 'holding power'   In addition to the natural increase in population and the effect of immigration, two other factors have played a not insignificant part in the school population increase. There have been unconcerted moves to raise the legal minimum school-leaving age. In general, it has been raised to fifteen years, although in certain states, either by law or the arrangement of examinations, it is effectively sixteen. The other phenomenon of importance has been an increase in the 'holding power' of secondary schools, particularly noticeable during the sixties. More young people of secondary school age voluntarily remaining at secondary school for five or six years, instead of three or four, have accentuated the accommodation and teacher-supply problems facing educational administrators. The actual percentage of males of seventeen years of age or over still in school in 1955 was 12·5, in 1960 20·7 per cent, and in 1970 it had reached 31·7 per cent. Figures for females were lower (7·0 in 1955, 23·7 per cent in 1970).[10] It is absolutely clear that what has been happening in Australian education has been a steady, significantly marked increase in the number of young people wanting a full secondary education; its effects on tertiary education have already become apparent.

Thus the number of schools has expanded greatly, particularly at secondary level, and the general size of existing schools has grown remarkably. Without doubt the states inherited a lag in school construction from the depression era and the war; early post-war expansion was hindered by shortages of building materials and labour and, when these had been overcome, by a dearth of finance. However, every cloud has a silver lining, and the position was helped by experiments in new building media and techniques and, more recently, by some financial assistance from the Commonwealth government. School furniture has been modernised, much obsolete plant replaced, and special facilities

provided. Although complaints about school accommodation
are still heard with regular monotony, in all fairness it must be
admitted that much progress has been made. Architecturally,
and for facilities and equipment, today's Australian school com-
pares more than well with the school of 1945.

More money for education   A second effect of the rapid
enrolment increases is the total amount of finance which each
state has had to devote to education. This came, not only from
the need for money to acquire additional school sites and build
new schools and additional classrooms, but also from the need
to pay higher salaries to a larger body of teachers and to train
more young people for entry to the teaching profession. Government finance comes from two sources: running expenses are
usually met from consolidated revenue funds, which consist of
income tax reimbursements from the Commonwealth, revenue
receipts, and indirect taxation by the states (for example,
taxes on poker machines, stamp duty on property transfers,
and   probate   duty),   while   capital   outlay   is   met   from
Commonwealth-raised loan funds, over which amount the state
treasurers wrangle annually with the federal treasurer. Owing
to the states' voluntary surrender of direct income taxing powers
to the Commonwealth during wartime, they are now dependent
on the Commonwealth for the vast majority of their funds. In
view of the effects of inflation on money values, little is gained
by citing the amounts year by year devoted to educational purposes, or for that matter by comparing percentage increases (see,
however, tables on pp 37–9). What can be said is that the size
of funds devoted to education has increased enormously since
1945 and the percentage of total state expenditure on education
as compared with other social services has likewise climbed
dramatically. Three points of caution, however, seem necessary.
First, until the early sixties independent schools (whose enrolments, as has been noted, were increasing in a dramatic manner
also) received no substantial direct aid from state or Commonwealth, and in particular the position of Catholic schools was—

and still is—precarious. In the second place, educational expenditure as a percentage of the gross national product has risen, but still remains depressed when compared with many leading developed countries. Third, some informed observers are convinced that there has to be an upper limit to educational expenditure vis-à-vis other social services, and that the relative financial honeymoon that Australian schools, universities and colleges have enjoyed may well end, since hospitals, pensions and other important government commitments are in sore need of financial supplementation.

TABLES SHOWING GROWTH IN AUSTRALIAN EDUCATION

(Many assert that the phenomena B to F could have been materially assisted by greater Commonwealth expenditure (G) on education.)

(A)

POPULATION

Census Figures and Estimates		No of Annual Births in Australia	
1901	3,773,800	1932	120,000
1921	5,435,700	1945	160,000
1933	6,629,800	1950	190,000
1954	8,986,500	1955	208,000
1966	11,550,500	1960	230,000
1970	12,713,400 (est)	1965	223,000
		1970	257,000
		1971	276,000

(B)

SCHOOL ENROLMENTS

Government Schools		Non-Government Schools	
1901	638,000	1901	149,000
1921	879,000	1921	199,000
1951	1,023,300	1951	325,000
1961	1,663,000	1961	527,000
1965	1,857,000 (567, 500 Sec)	1970	608,000
1971	2,196,500 (745,100 Sec)		

(C)
EDUCATIONAL EXPENDITURE ($m)
*Estimated for all Australia, Public and
Private, Current and Capital*

Year	$m
1949	74
1955	224
1960	426
1965	737
1970	1,287

(D)
TEACHERS IN TRAINING
Government Schools

Year	Total	Primary	Secondary
1960	15,460	8,202	7,258
1965	23,606	10,074	13,532
1970	36,370	14,435	21,935

(E)
TEACHERS
Government Schools
(1901 14,500   1921 26,900)

Year	Total	Primary	Secondary
1950	34,964	26,686	8,278
1965	74,795	45,670	29,125
1970	95,041	54,481	40,560

Of which females:

	51,805	34,729	17,076

Non-Government Schools

1901	8,300
1921	8,800
1951	11,300
1965	22,000
1970	24,000

(F)
RATIO OF STUDENTS TO TEACHERS
All Government

Year	Schools	Primary	Secondary
1960	28.7	32.1	21.6
1965	25.0	28.9	19.0
1970	23.0	27.1	17.6

(G) COMMONWEALTH GOVERNMENT EDUCATIONAL EXPENDITURE ($m)

Year	Grants to States			Cash Benefits (Scholarships)	Goods and Services		
	Curr	Cap	Total		Curr	Cap	Total
1960	9.7	5.5	15.2	8.2	6.8	3.4	10.2
1964	21.0	12.8	33.8	10.4	14.7	9.2	23.9
1967	38.8	40.1	78.9	27.3	24.0	11.2	35.2
1971	103.3	74.4	177.3	45.3	57.4	18.5	75.9

Increase
1960–71	965%	1,245%	1,066%	452%	744%	544%	644%

Sources: *Education News*; Commonwealth Office of Education, *Statistics of Australian Education for 1960 and Earlier Years*, Bulletin no 17, 1962; *Commonwealth Year Book* (various years); Radford, W. C. (Comp) *The Non-Government Schools of Australia* (Melbourne, 1953); *Review of Education in Australia 1955–1962* (Melbourne, 1964); Fitzgerald, R. T., 'Emerging Issues in the Seventies', *Quarterly Review of Australian Education* 5/3 (September 1972); Wheelwright, E. L. (ed) *Higher Education in Australia* (Melbourne, 1965), 336

Recruiting more teachers The considerable expansion in the provision of trained teachers has been noted briefly; at the same time contention has surrounded the means and efficacy of this programme. Certainly it is true that the percentage of funds for teacher education has lagged, since other necessities seemed of greater urgency to administrators. Nevertheless, the number of teachers' colleges has risen, and the number of their products has increased. Similarly, the number of teachers trained at universities and special institutes has shown an increase, rises being especially marked during the latter portion of the 1960s. As already stressed, this increased supply has made some improvement to the pupil/teacher ratio (that is, to decreased class size). It would be a considerably better picture had not attempts been made to make teachers available for special work, like the care of handicapped children and for schools in Papua-New Guinea.

The real difficulty in the recruitment of additional teachers has been demographic. The upsurge in school enrolments called for a response from the small generations born during the depression era.[11] The introduction of the Commonwealth Scholarship Scheme (by which fees and living allowances have been paid to a fair percentage of university attenders) has, until quite recently, further diminished the recruitment pool of teachers. Several methods of encouraging more young people to prepare for teaching were tried during the period being reviewed. These included 'teaching scholarships' in some states to keep prospective recruits at school until matriculation. Several states have actively recruited teachers from overseas systems, while others have employed untrained or insufficiently trained persons. Teachers' salaries have been forced upwards through the shortage and as a result of the favourable bargaining position in which teachers' unions found themselves. But the supply position is changing: whereas in the early fifties almost any recruit of even minimum academic calibre was accepted for a teachers' college place, now there is considerable selectivity in an uncertain economic climate where demand for college places is extremely strong and competitive. Further, there is evidence of demand slowly being satisfied, since several categories of specialist secondary teacher are in fair supply, even if a shortage still exists in the mathematics-science fields.

Expanding educational bureaucracy   It might well be expected that, with so large an increase in the size of the expanded schooling operation, there would be a plethora of administrators for purposes of supervising, directing, planning and those other activities which seem to find their place under the general banner of administration and organisation. It *is* true that the number of inspectors, directors and other senior officers has increased. There has been an increase in research and guidance personnel, too, but the *percentage* of the education vote spent on administration (salaries, accommodation, ancillary staff) has not risen markedly. It is probably true that the average age of administrators is lower, that they have more job mobility, and certainly higher academic attainments than was the case even thirty years ago. The educational administrator today is more of a professional than his forebear, and he brings a more modern and perhaps critical view to each problem, even if he is caught up in a more bureaucratic machine than hitherto.

Rural and technical education   The stress on providing as equally as possible for the country child and for his city cousin has already been mentioned. Although in the post-war years it has been the cities which have had the larger expansion, several developments in rural education have been of importance. Correspondence education has been one of these: emphasis has been placed on more varied facilities for the isolated secondary pupil and on the opening of 'schools of the air'. There has also been expansion in agricultural education, although for the time being the zenith of interest in the land appears to have passed. Several independent secondary schools for boys have also specialised in agricultural courses. Rather more urgent has been meeting the demand for technical education, and in this direction rural areas have not been neglected. In New South Wales a separate Department of Technical Education was established in 1949, and more regional technical colleges established in country towns. Nevertheless the pace of technical development has been so swift that the majority of funds available have been allotted to urban developments, particularly in areas with heavy concentrations of industry. This has been done despite the fact that, for most of the post-war period, technical education has been out of the public eye, and indeed frequently enough called the 'Cinderella' of Australian education. This can hardly be said to be any longer the case, what with the establishment of the New South Wales University of Technology (later called the University of NSW and now one of the biggest universities in Australia), the Victoria Institute of Colleges and expansion of similar kinds in most other states, following the recommendations of the Martin Report of 1964 (see later, Chapter 4).

Educating adults   The public has accorded even less attention to adult education. The Workers' Educational Association and university organisations (such as the Sydney University

Department of Tutorial Classes) have long existed for the purpose of promoting and encouraging various forms of adult education, and their budgets have expanded in keeping with the times.
Perhaps the best known encouragements to adult education have
been the *Current Affairs Bulletin* (originally a wartime army
venture), and in northern New South Wales the community
development activities of the Extension Department of the University of New England. But, in general, insufficient impetus
for comprehensive adult education programmes seems to be
forthcoming. Similarly, the expansion of parent organisations
connected with schools and educational questions generally has
been considerable, but perhaps equally lacking in decisive impact. True, there is greater public interest in educational questions
today, if one can judge from the amount of newspaper space
devoted to them, and the concern shown for educational policy
by political parties, but actual parental involvement in the schools
their children attend still seems generally limited to raising
funds for additional equipment over and above the basic supplies
provided by 'the department'. Not that parents are really encouraged to develop an interest in the educational questions
relating to their school; indeed, the opposite is often true.
Teachers, principals and administrators alike only minimally
encourage involvement of this kind. Far too often parental interest and energy are restricted to arrangements for the next
school fête.

Independent schools   Rather more parental interest, and
certainly more public heat, is generated either in relation to the
existence of independent schools or their (generally financial)
relationship to the state schools. Since the mid-fifties, the
Liberal-Country Party Coalition government (in office from
1949 to 1972 in Canberra) has provided grants or loans to independent schools for a variety of needs. Admittedly, many of the
schemes—which prove very helpful, especially as catchers of the
Catholic vote—have been used to assist government schools as
well. Among these have been funds for school libraries and the

building of additional science laboratories. But they have raised again the old question of 'state aid'. Among certain sectors of the population, this renewed aid is viewed with alarm, either on religious grounds (since the vast majority of independent school places are for Catholic children) or social ones (money has not been distributed on a needs basis). However, controversies aside, the independent schools *have* had heavy demands made upon them and they have found the recruitment of staff equally as difficult as have government schools. Thus, Federal aid has been very helpful; in some cases it has constituted a lifeline, particularly in the case of the poorer Catholic parochial school. Perhaps the most difficult situation has been in urban Victoria, where many Catholic migrants have settled. The Catholic hierarchy responded to the problems presented to them with commendable vigour. Church teachers' colleges were expanded, and new schools built, but the problem persists, undoubtedly accentuated by the fall in vocations to teaching orders and the consequent need to recruit lay teachers with their higher salary levels. It is as yet too early to determine whether the Labor Party's 1972 Federal election victory (largely the result of its heavier vote in the key states of New South Wales and Victoria) may have been due to a return of Catholic voters to their traditional allegiance. Certainly the Labor Party no longer opposes state aid.

Pre-schools and ACER   To conclude this section of discussion of the expansion over more than two decades, reference might be made first to pre-schools and the tardiness with which they have developed, and second to the expanding role of the Australian Council for Educational Research (ACER). Most states have been loath to commit themselves to a full-scale preschool system, and as a result most activity in this area has been confined to voluntary and charitable organisations. It is understandable that departments of education have felt fully committed to providing for those children of the age of compulsory school attendance and beyond. Nevertheless, there is increasing pressure, both from the community in general and also from pre-school educators themselves, for more government assistance for, and involvement in, pre-school or nursery provision.

By way of contrast, ACER has enjoyed considerable expansion. It is autonomous, but is financed by governments. Since its inception (before World War II) it has played a prominent part in developing thinking and new ideas in Australian education. Originally, the organisation was known for its psychological and test services, and for its role in publishing research reports on aspects of Australian education. The previous concentration on psychological and intelligence tests, which helped its financial resources considerably, has now widened to embrace the research and development of new types of attainment tests; at the same time its publications, relatively popular as well as esoteric, are now more diverse. It has a very good library, an expanded staff (located in Melbourne), and is now involved in numerous curriculum reform projects. ACER's reputation grows higher each year.

CHANGING EMPHASES IN EDUCATIONAL ADMINISTRATION

It should not be thought, however, that Australia's education systems have merely expanded in the last two or three decades: in certain respects change has been as important as expansion.

Attempts at decentralisation   State centralisation of educational administration is, as has already been shown, a feature of Australian history; indeed, centralisation *per se* may well be an important characteristic of Australian development generally. However, the tendency towards centralisation has bred some interesting and significant changes during the period under consideration. Unquestionably, the first of these is the attempt to decentralise educational administration in New South Wales and Queensland. The division of the former state into administrative areas for purposes of school administration had its beginnings in 1948 with the appointment of a director of education to an experimental area in the south-west. The director had no pre-

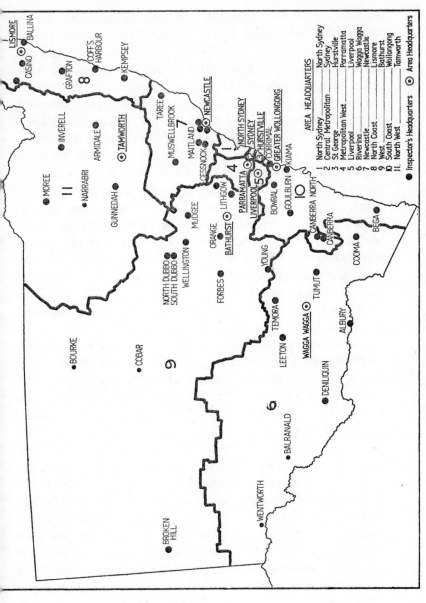

Fig 2   Department of Education directorates in New South Wales

rogative in formulating policy; his task was to implement it. Being closer to the scene, he could implement policy with greater judgement, and more appropriately, so the theory ran. In 1952, the scheme was judged successful (although on what criteria has never been made clear) and other areas were designated. At the present time, the scheme has been extended so as to include even Sydney, and the state is divided into what are now called 'directorates' (see Fig 2). The plan followed has been to decentralise progressively, in that details of administration have gradually been moved over to area offices. The work of directors has been assisted by the appointment of clerical staff, area advisers, supervisors and secondary inspectors, in addition to the existing corps of district inspectors. A somewhat similar situation has developed in Queensland, where the necessity for some regional organisation was obvious because of the huge size of the state. Claims are made that decentralisation of function makes for better decisions and for more appropriate public relations, and thus leaves the central administration more time for considering important state-wide policy decisions.

Rural school consolidation   Reference has also been made to the tendency for the consolidation of schools. Perhaps Tasmania, the smallest state, was one of the first, in the 1930s, to attempt consolidation by the closing of small rural schools and the use of public transport to take students to larger centres.[12] Somewhat later, consolidated schools started to appear in the more sparsely settled areas of western Victoria. New South Wales has never had a deliberate policy of consolidation, but inevitably the advent of efficient bus transportation has ensured diminution in the number of one-teacher rural schools. Governments now have large annual votes to meet transport costs, for consolidation has become popular in all states. Originally, it should be remembered, the rural school was established to ensure uniformity of education, because 'uniformity begets equality of educational opportunity' and without this 'competition would become capricious and unfair'. In the thirties P. R. Cole was able

to argue that 'no system [*sic*] in the world gives greater encouragement to boys and girls of moderate cirumstances who may be
possessed of talent'.[13] More recently, the same centralised systems
apparently argue that equality of educational opportunity can be
even more equal by means of consolidation.

Scientific administration   Another important change has
been an increased emphasis on more scientific administration.
Sir Harold Wyndham, who became Director-General of Education in New South Wales in the early fifties, had obtained his
EdD from Stanford University and had been the state's first
research officer. He did not come to his high position through
the traditional channel of long experience as headmaster and
inspector of schools (although, for a short time, he was a school
inspector). During Wyndham's régime the Division of Research,
Guidance and Adjustment, which he had in effect begun, became
two professional divisions—Research and Planning, and Guidance and Adjustment—both bringing scientific and professional
expertise to bear on problems of student counselling, suitable
school placement for students, school planning and a multitude
of research questions. Other state departments have established
similar organisations, while the teaching of educational administration by universities has become an important part of graduate
work in education'. Centres for research in learning and instruction, and measurement and evaluation within the New South
Wales Department are perhaps the most recent further developments in bringing newly discovered, world-wide expertise to bear
on school problems.

Curriculum revision   One of the important functions of
research units is the management of curriculum revision and
adaptation which has changed markedly in nature over the
period. It was long the custom in a centralised education system
for curricular statements to be issued as it were by fiat and to
remain unchanged for many years. But increasingly teachers,
lecturers and professional specialists have become involved in
regular reviews of courses of study. It is now far more common

for a curriculum to be reviewed and revised in sections at regular intervals. This policy of continuous revision involves a high degree of teacher and researcher participation. The result has been the earlier introduction of new methods and approaches, as for example, in the cuisenaire method of teaching mathematics and new approaches to art education, and also more suitable means of curricular evaluation. Particular attention has been paid to more appropriate courses of study for below-average secondary students and, since in almost all states there have been major reviews of secondary education arrangements, it has been possible to adjust the curricular offerings to the broader spectrum of ability now represented by the increased secondary school population.

In summary, then, considerable change has taken place in school curricula throughout Australia. This has affected the non-government as well as the government school, as in secular subject matter the former, because of public examination necessities, usually follows where the state leads. In a sense, it is perhaps the best example of the power of centralisation, for until very recently the non-government schools in Australia have not, in general, been noted for their sense of experiment.

In-service education for teachers   In-service education for teachers has also received heavy and welcome emphasis. The opportunity for teachers with a teachers' college education to gain a university degree by evening or external university study has been expanded: the University of New England, for instance, provides external teaching for the same courses as are taught internally for arts and economics degrees, and the diploma in education. Most of that university's external students are teachers. The scheme has operated since 1955. Even before that the teachers' colleges had offered voluntary refresher, or 'post-college', courses in vacations and these were quite well patronised. Most state departments provide a variety of in-service-type publications and a number run courses especially designed to meet the need for further in-service education. Conferences of principals of schools, subject masters, rural school-teachers, and so on are held regularly, and often at conference centres maintained by a particular department of education. Through these meetings, innovative ideas are disseminated, policies explained and ideas exchanged.

Concern for the disadvantaged One of the important milestones in Australian education in the last few years has been the change in attitude towards the handicapped. Although in some places and at some times the changed attitude degenerates into sickly sentiment, in general the prosperous Australian community has dealt fairly and squarely with the problem. Increased public desire to help those handicapped in various ways no doubt reflects a world-wide trend, but in Australia it is in keeping with what might be described as a national ethos of providing equal opportunity, or a 'fair go', as widely as possible. Despite other and heavy calls on limited resources, centralised state administrations, often spurred on by community action, have done a considerable amount to provide teachers and improve facilities. Opportunity classes for slow-learning children and itinerant remedial teachers (for those children of normal intelligence, who are for some reason retarded in school attainment) have been provided, even if on an insufficient scale, and the moderately mentally retarded child, once considered ineducable, has been assisted by special schools and classes. In New South Wales, these latter are known as Opportunity F classes and many are established in centres maintained by voluntary organisations. Special classes for deaf children also exist, Opportunity D classes in the same state being established especially to cater for the victims of the 1940–1 rubella epidemic when the connection with deafness became known. Victoria has led the way in training teachers of the deaf.

In Victoria also, legislation makes education for handicapped children compulsory and subsidies are provided for various forms of care, while several states emphasise providing a near to normal situation for the education of young people with handicaps.

D

Commonwealth assistance is forthcoming in a number of areas: a rehabilitation scheme and sheltered workshops for handicapped people are administered by the Department of Social Services, nursing assistance for severe cases and free hearing aids for people under twenty-one from the Commonwealth Acoustic Laboratories, and, under the States Grants (Independent Schools) Act, per capita grants for handicapped children's schools not run by state authorities. One area in which progress has been slow is in the provision of specialist courses of teacher education; the need, for example, for well-trained remedial teachers has long been a cause for concern, as it has been for other categories such as teachers for the deaf and blind, but the situation is slowly improving. Universities are also providing more courses in special education; for a long time the brightest light on the Australian horizon was the Remedial Education Centre at the University of Queensland and its work of providing special intensive courses for remedial teachers.

Reference has already been made to classes provided for the education of gifted children although, unfortunately, these classes, and many other types of provision for atypical children, are often limited to the larger and more populous centres. Another problem of concern—and still to be properly resolved—is the education of aboriginal children, a matter in which Australia's record is far from good.

Concern over the existence of unequal opportunity in education is again on the increase, and the change in this direction can be clearly seen in much of the publicity by university students. The Australian Union of Students, not content with highlighting inequalities at the tertiary level, has, of very recent years, drawn the community's attention to many other inequalities still extant in the case of aboriginal children, migrants, rural deprivation as compared with the cities, slum populations, and other groups. To match this renaissance of concern there is undoubtedly a widening community appreciation of talent (which no longer is seen as merely academic) and a considerable number of new initiatives (frequently under-valued) by departments of education to encourage greater opportunity.

The comprehensive secondary school   One set of such initiatives has concerned the reform of the secondary school, since the solely academic high school is no longer ubiquitous today. Rather, there has been a swing to the comprehensive high school in most systems. To the extent that university entrance requirements will allow, the secondary school has broadened its base, its curriculum and intake, and now is generally accepted as a vehicle of necessary general education for all adolescents. In New South Wales, for instance, the Wyndham Report of 1957 recommended comprehensive schooling, an extra secondary year and a core curriculum, among a lengthy list of general recommendations for change;[14] it was implemented in 1962. In that year, too, a special committee in Queensland was established to recommend changes which, when effected, were equally far reaching. Much the same could be said for reorganised secondary education in other states, and at a time when the sheer demand for more secondary education places was reaching a distinct peak.

Part and parcel of the changes in the secondary school was concern over examinations which had long dominated the secondary systems in what many felt was an unfortunate way. Although exams have often been seen as fair (in an equalising sort of way), the post-war years have seen two rather contradictory trends. There has been a trend away from formal, external, public examinations of the traditional type, and their replacement by accrediting, new forms of assessment and special standardised examinations. At the same time, the eager Australian penchant for gaining paper qualifications has in no way diminished, so that to a large extent the stress on examination success has remained. Admittedly, these generalisations are broad, and perhaps anticipate the final outcomes of several new examining and assessing procedures on which experiments are currently proceeding.

SOME MAJOR SHIFTS IN EMPHASIS

Thus far, emphasis has been placed separately on features which shows expansion or development, and those which exhibit change. It is now necessary to review others which reflect both expansion and change. The first, and perhaps most significant of these in the post-war period, is Commonwealth participation in education.

The Commonwealth and education　　As has been stressed, constitutionally education is a state matter in Australia but it is clear that, while the constitution remains constant, Australia and Australian life have changed greatly in the decades since 1939. If for the outside observer it is difficult to understand the great social changes that have taken place, in many ways it is equally as difficult for the Australian to comprehend them. His is a country whose population has all but doubled, which has thrown off a colonial syndrome and now stands tall as a nation, which has grown rich and boasts one of the highest living standards in the world.

If events and changes have moved with great swiftness in a short time, the role of the Commonwealth government has changed even more. Australians still look to government for action, as in colonial days, but it is the Federal government which now has the money, and hence the real power. For the states, still jealous of their sovereign rights, are but mendicants to Canberra when it comes to financial resources.

By 1955 Commonwealth participation in education was already heavy. The Office of Education found itself with much work of an international liaison nature (for example, the United Nations Technical Assistance Scheme and UNESCO), matters in connection with the immigration programme, the Commonwealth Scholarship Scheme, and education in the territories.[15]

As early as 1951 the Commonwealth made emergency grants to the states for university finances, and again in and after 1957 with the publication of the Murray Report which recommended massive Federal aid for state universities.[16] The importance of this move was emphasised by the establishment of the Australian Universities Commission, a Commonwealth government instrumentality, in 1959. The extent of aid to tertiary education was high-lighted by the even more far-reaching provisions of the Martin Report in 1964, which advised the spread of Commonwealth assistance to new forms of tertiary education.[17]

For significance, this change and expansion in tertiary education was matched by the venture of the Commonwealth—which has already been mentioned—into 'state-aid' for independent schools, begun in 1956 and expanded considerably during the sixties.

Expansion and change in tertiary education　　The two changes mentioned above were symptomatic of a greater commitment to education, both by government and the community at large. The size of the commitment is reflected in the greatly increased demand for tertiary education. With the universities of Sydney, New South Wales, Melbourne and Queensland climbing to enrolments of about 16,000 or more, and the opening of new institutions such as Macquarie University (in Sydney), Monash and La Trobe in Melbourne, and Flinders (Adelaide), and the planning of second universities in Brisbane (Griffith) and Perth (Murdoch), as well as discussions about a fourth Victorian university, another in New South Wales, and the opening of James Cook University at Townsville in North Queensland, the extent of pressure on traditional forms of higher education is exemplified.

Among the university developments of the post-war years have been the merging of Canberra University College with the Australian National University in 1960 and the granting of autonomy to the New England University College in late 1953. The latter now has five faculties (including rural science), caters for many students preparing to be teachers and also provides external degree and diploma courses which are equivalent in status to internal awards. The dearth of rural universities points to the concentration of population in the cities, as the only other university outside the capital cities is James Cook University. The Australian National University, as its name suggests, caters on a national basis in the rapidly growing Federal capital, and other new universities have been established in the larger centres of population, rather than sited to serve the countryman. However, the growth reflects the increasing educational conscience of the Australian community and the realisation that higher education is highly advantageous in a competitive, increasingly complex society.

Yet growth has not merely been in terms of expansion, for diversification (or change) has been manifest: Commonwealth assistance, based on Martin Report recommendations, for technical education, teachers' colleges, and a new concept of tertiary colleges (subsequently called colleges of advanced education) has been most important. Diversification is seen in terms of a greater supply of technicians and technologists, and there has been rather more than a suspicion that Federal government thinking has seen the allocation of funds to tertiary education in terms of national and economic development, that is, education as investment. By widening the higher education system, the selectivity of universities seems assured; with massive Federal aid and bodies like the Australian Universities Commission to control financial allocations, effective autonomy seems a thing of the past.

Preparation and supervision of teachers   In the case of the states, change associated with growth has had a major impact in the modification of the inspection system of teachers. If it is true that, to a large extent, this modification has been forced upon authorities by the sheer growth in size of the teaching force, in effect it tends to lighten the authoritarian role of the administrator. The changes made in the various states have been quite far reaching, and represent an enhancement of teachers' professional standing, but more change is likely.

Teacher education has gone through a traumatic period since about 1950. At that date the term 'teacher training' was still in common use, but 'teacher education', while not universal today, is sufficiently used to indicate a rather broader approach to the preparation of teachers. Teacher preparation has not been the recipient of liberal funds, but by the early 1950s vigorous efforts were being made to increase the number of trainees. There were about 5,500 in training in 1951, whereas by 1960 the figure stood at 15,000 and by 1970 had reached 36,370.[18] With fresh ideas college curricula have, in some cases, shown radical change. The most recent move has been towards the incorporation of teacher preparation programmes in multi-purpose institutions such as colleges of advanced education. Some universities have supplemented or changed their traditional role of preparing graduates for teaching through diplomas by introducing BEd programmes, in which academic and professional preparation take place concurrently rather than end on.

School libraries   One remarkable aspect of development over the past two or three decades has been the development of school libraries. The Pitt-Munn Report of the 1930s castigated the state of library services in Australia; not only have free public libraries blossomed in the intervening years, but schools have developed libraries which range from the still meagre to the very fine. Teacher-librarians have been appointed to many of the larger schools, Federal funds have assisted the construction of new library buildings in schools and library subsidies have helped to stock the new shelves. When this kind of development is considered alongside the change in teaching methods in schools, whereby student research has become an important ingredient of the approach to learning, the significance of development in this area becomes manifest.

THE STYLE OF ADMINISTRATION

State bureaucracies today   The six Australian states show rather more similarity in their educational organisation than one might expect, since they have had authority in the field for many years, and Commonwealth participation, although growing rapidly, is still relatively minor except in tertiary education. In fact, the states have adopted basically the same or similar organisation and control. Although New South Wales exemplifies the administrative pattern in many ways and will be described here as an example, it is atypical in at least one major respect, in that it has a separate Department of Technical Education although, with the Department of Education, it is under the control of the same minister.

The State Department in New South Wales assumes responsibility for primary and secondary education, facets of teacher education, some adult education and leisure-time activities. Its work is supplemented by the Technical Education Department, mentioned above, and by bodies like the Advanced Education Board and the Universities Board. The Department of Education has a head office in Sydney and a number of area offices, each in an administrative area or directorate. Figure 2 on page 45 shows the division of the state into the eleven administrative regions. Each area has a director of education who is responsible for the supervision, through district inspectors, of teachers, the operation of schools within the area, and for the allocation of funds to carry out pre-determined programmes. Important policy matters are determined at 'head office', by State Cabinet or Parliament in Sydney, and finance is provided from the annual state budget. The arrangement is a form of partial decentralisation, policy implementation rather than policy itself.

The administrative pattern of the New South Wales Department is shown in Fig 3. It is complicated and, to the uninformed observer, heavy with bureaucratic machinery. However, the percentage of state funds spent on administrative costs has always been kept low (about 3 per cent of the total) and the machinery has to cope with a system of very large order, some 811,000 children, 2,400 schools and 36,000 teachers. Under the director-general, whose annual budget runs to over $450m (Australian currency: $AUST 1 = approx $US 1.30 or £0.50 sterling) and who is permanent head of the department, the administration is organised into appropriate divisions (properties, finance, teacher

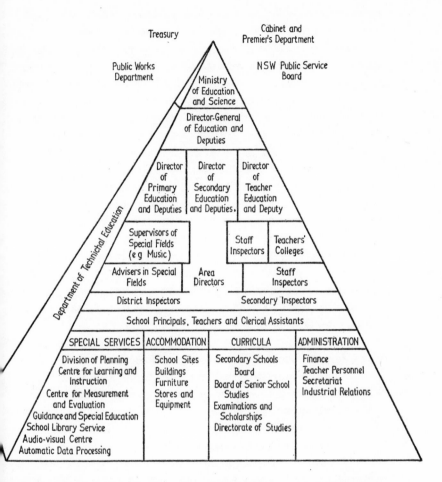

Fig 3 Administrative machinery of a state education system (New South Wales). The bureaucratic pyramid is supported by many centres, divisions, branches and other offices. The third face of the pyramid is represented by miscellaneous Department of Education and Science activities, eg NSW Universities Board, Advanced Education Board. Policy proposals emerging from the edifice are sometimes clouded by the attitudes expressed by the other departments shown

personnel, examinations and scholarships, automatic data processing, etc). There is a separate director for primary and for
secondary schools, with appropriate assistant directors, and a
director of teacher education and his deputy. The vast amount
of professional work is conducted by a corps of inspectors of
schools whose actual work of regular inspection of schools is
now diminished with the introduction of more professional
responsibility for school principals and teaching staff. Still, inspection is necessary if a teacher desires promotion, which is
determined on a state-wide basis. Schools as such are not inspected as regularly as they once were. Most inspectors of
secondary subjects operate from head office, but there are some
secondary inspectors appointed to assist directors of education
in the areas, and others (the more senior and efficient) are staff
inspectors whose general task is to assist the director of secondary
education on special matters. Primary inspectors each have a
district within an area, except for staff inspectors who may, or
may not, be attached to head office. The inspectorial staff serves
as a communication path to and from the schools: a high school
like that at Finley, for example, in south-western New South
Wales communicates with head office via the Deniliquin inspec-
torate, thence to the Riverina Area Directorate located at Wagga
Wagga, thence to Sydney. The idea of decentralisation, however,
is that most matters can be dealt with either by the inspector at
Deniliquin or by the director of education or one of his inspectorial assistants at Wagga Wagga.

Besides the organisation mentioned above, there are a number
of specialist professional bodies. For example, the Division of
Guidance and Special Education has school counsellors and
district guidance officers to arrange group and individual testing
of students and provide counselling, careers advisers to give
vocational advice, and also provide liaison between schools and
commerce and industry. Vocational guidance is also available
to secondary school students via the officers of the Department
of Labour and Industry. The seventeen categories of classes for

over 28,000 atypical children are also handled by the Division.

The Division of Planning, under its director, comprises an economic planning section concerned mainly with the demand for, and supply of, educational resources; a demographic planning unit which, for instance, plans the placement of primary students in secondary schools; an information section, and a survey section which undertakes various kinds of administrative research and surveys. The two educational research centres, already mentioned (see p 47), are attached to the Director of Planning: the Centre for Research in Learning and Instruction is concerned with analysing questions of practical classroom applicability in relation to learning capabilities and experiences, while the Centre for Research in Measurement and Evaluation seeks to develop procedures for assessing student achievement and aptitudes in both primary and secondary schools. Closely associated is a directorate of studies, responsible for developing curricula throughout the whole school system, and advising the directors of primary and secondary education, the Secondary Schools Board and the Board of Senior School Studies on curriculum questions.[19] In a system as large as that of New South Wales, there is no doubt that a corps of professional staff is a necessary adjunct to the usual inspectorial, clerical and upper administrative echelons. 'Boffins' or 'back-room boys' they might be called; their work is intricate, important and indispensable. Arrangements in other states along similar lines owe a large amount to the foresight shown by the forward planners in New South Wales.

One feature of this provision for specialist professional services is that it tends to reinforce the generally held idea that, despite the efforts at decentralisation, so much is still done at the centre. It is therefore hard to deny that the Australian states basically still have centralised education systems, since many of the day-to-day problems and most of the policy making are still concentrated in the capital cities. The main criticisms levelled at this situation are the insignificance felt by the individual teacher in such a large and impersonal system, the overlooking of individual needs in the machinery of centralised decision making, restrictions of centrally devised courses of study, the external examination system, and the inspectorial system. However, as we have seen, in recent years the last three complaints have certainly carried less weight.

Non-government schools About one of every four children attending school in Australia is enrolled in a non-government school, and of these about 80 per cent attend Roman Catholic schools. Often called 'private' or 'independent' rather than 'non-government', these schools are generally church-based, although with resurgence in government aid to non-government schools a handful of new independent schools has been established, generally on the basis of promoting new, progressive curricular and methodological approaches. However, the majority of schools in the private sector follows closely the secular courses of study as in government schools, largely because of the necessity for their pupils to sit for external public examinations. In 1971 a total of 2,180 non-government schools were in operation, and of these 1,781 were under the auspices of the Roman Catholic Church.[20] The Church of England controlled 108, 33 were Presbyterian and 19 Methodist sponsored. Other schools are run by the Seventh Day Adventist Church, Lutherans and Jews, while there were 127 schools classified as undenominational, although many of these have links with a particular Christian denomination, or claim a Christian basis for their educational philosophy. New South Wales has the most non-government schools (790), with Victoria next (581) and Queensland third (342). Other states, with lesser populations, claim smaller numbers, but on the basis of the number of schools to school-age children in each state or territory, Canberra has the highest ratio, with Victoria next. These schools are staffed by about 24,000 teachers of whom some 6,000 are employed on a part-time basis; enrolments, exceeding 600,000, are about evenly divided between boys and girls. An increasing tendency is for these schools, once almost exclusively single-sex schools, to move towards co-education. In the more exclusive non-government schools the pupil/teacher ratio is very satisfactory, indeed favourable, while in the poorer parochial Catholic schools it gives continual cause for concern. In some states private schools are subject to inspection, in others their teachers must be registered, and in still others they are inspected on request.

There would seem to be two main problems surrounding non-government schools. The first, and most publicised, is their financial position. All charge fees; in the better known, more exclusive schools the fees are high, particularly for boarders, while in the Roman Catholic sector fees vary with the type of school. Catholic school fees are usually lower, and in parish schools it is not unknown for fees to be waived in necessitous circumstances. Since the passing of the 'free, compulsory and secular' Acts in the late nineteenth century and until recent reversals of government policy, no funds from government had been available to non-government schools. However, starting with the Commonwealth government's decision to grant interest-free loans to independent schools in the Australian Capital Territory, political pressures have encouraged governments to reintroduce certain aid measures. These have been directed largely to assuaging Catholic claims that, for their schools to continue to operate (and hence take an intolerable pressure off government schools), heavy financial assistance is necessary. Aid by way of per capita grants and capital grants for new buildings (science blocks and secondary school libraries) are cases in point.

The second problem is that of the supply and training of teachers for non-government schools. Traditionally, Roman Catholic schools have employed members of religious orders, and this has saved substantial salary costs, but the dearth of vocations, together with heavy increases in young Catholics of school age, has forced the hierarchy to employ many more lay teachers, with inevitable results. Special training programmes have attempted to meet the supply needs. In other independent schools, with improved salaries the position is not so acute, but the trend here has been to provide more pre- and in-service education for teachers, rather than rely, as has been traditional, on untrained graduates. Two teachers' colleges, meeting some of the needs of Protestant independent schools, exist in Melbourne and Sydney.

Thus it would seem fair to assert that Australia has not only six systems of state schools, but more than one system of independent schools as well. Indeed, many would assert that the non-government schools hardly comprise a system or systems, because of the traditional lack of cohesion among the constituent parts. This is hardly fair, since the principals of many independent schools have joined forces, even if loosely, in the Headmasters Conference of the Independent Schools of Australia and the Association of Heads of Independent Girls' Schools of Australia. In addition, there is a National Council of Independent Schools representing all independent schools and dedicated to promoting their interests. In the post-war years, therefore, the non-government sector, although not without problems, has strengthened itself and appears, despite growth in the government sector, firmly fixed in the Australian educational ladder.

A NATIONAL OBJECTIVE AND STYLE?

By the time the Australian young person of today has reached the university, college of advanced education, technical or teachers' college, he has climbed a lengthy educational ladder, built up in sections over a period of almost two hundred years. It seems as if the nineteenth-century task was the spread of elementary, or primary, education with the object of the spread of literacy in a basically urban settlement dependent largely on primary industry, but becoming increasingly familiar with elements of secondary industry which of necessity demanded more educated people. The first half of the present century saw the growth of secondary schools, first for an élite of talent, then for all. This 'equal opportunity' was not in all respects equal, but as time has passed the number of young men and women staying to high school graduation has increased, phenomenally since World War II. The second half of the century has seen—and will continue to see—the expansion of the third part of the ladder, tertiary education. Therefore, by the time our school student of the opening paragraph of Chapter 1 has ventured from basic geographical facts to the complexity of knowledge and understanding required in tertiary education institutions, he has probably also realised that Australians have always looked to the centre of things, to 'the government' for help. And, in a new world, they have always believed in a 'fair go'. Reflecting this epitome of the Australian attitude to life and the underdog, government has been largely concerned with the pursuit of greater social equality, to combat privilege, and to assist the common man, whether he be an old age pensioner, a rural worker, or a handicapped child. True, there have been times when, in the pursuit of war, or the benefits of affluence, these objectives have been temporarily submerged, when the pursuit of personal opportunity has loomed larger than political aims of greater social equality, and when economic growth has seemed more attainable than social justice. But the pendulum always swings back. Justice and equality through centralised government could well be the national objective and national style.

3
The School Ladder

HAVING traced the beginnings of the Australian educational systems and seen something of the way in which they have developed and are organised, it is now appropriate to look in rather more detail at the various sections of the educational ladder which has been created. Come, therefore, into the classroom, whether it be the traditional kind with four walls accommodating thirty to forty students, or airy new teaching spaces of the open or grouped kind, or a school of the air—one quite without walls. In this chapter we look at primary and secondary schools which operate on the basis of a three-term year beginning in February, with the long summer vacation being taken in January of each year. No tuition fees are charged in government schools but parents often meet expenses of uniforms, books and equipment. Such financial outlay is tax-deductible.

First, however, it is necessary to say a word about the nursery or pre-school, even though it is by no means yet common and is often conducted on a voluntary or fee-paying basis. The aim of nursery education for two-, three- or four-year-olds can probably be stated as health training and basic social adjustment. Stories, simple games, singing activities in very small groups, and play facilities help the children adjust to their fellows, while teachers also spend much time in promoting basic health training, correct nutrition (especially in depressed areas where government nursery schools are often to be found), sleep and rest. On the whole more four-year-olds attend pre-school than two-year-olds.[1]

PRIMARY SCHOOLS

Primary schooling in Australia extends from about the age of five to twelve years, although there are variations among the states: in Victoria, for example, children leave primary grades rather early, and in Queensland rather late. The classes for smaller children between five and seven or eight are sometimes called the infants' grades and may be given the nomenclature, as in South Australia, of preparatory, grade 1 and grade 2, or, as in New South Wales, of kindergarten, grade 1 and grade 2. They are almost invariably staffed by women teachers. The primary school proper then consists of grades 3–6 or 3–7 (see Fig. 4 on p 73). In some states and in larger centres special provision is made for dull and retarded children, either by classes for slow learners or by remedial teachers. However, there is still a distinct shortage of teachers specially trained for remedial work.

The infants' grades were probably the first rungs of the school ladder to be influenced by modern educational ideas from overseas. As a result, for many years the early classes of school life have been extremely vital and experimental. The basic aims of education at this level are the inculcation of simple and basic skills, knowledge and attitudes. Today there is much emphasis on creativity in the infants' classes, as well as the employment of the latest methods of teaching the basic skills, such as cuisenaire rods and well-known playway techniques. Reading skills are, of course, of supreme importance and before a child reaches grade 3 he is expected to be able to read quite competently. Writing skills are introduced shortly after reading is begun, and usually in a form of a simplified script. Much learning centres around themes (as, for example, 'our town', 'people who help us' and 'Christmas time for the world's children') and the use of a variety of teaching aids and materials is universal. The health instruction of the preschool is continued and extended, while physical education lessons and very simple games skills are taught regularly. The young child's sense of wonder is stimulated by stories, and by

E

lessons in natural science, although a much needed swing to simple general science (such as space exploration) is taking place. Particular emphasis is placed on art, simple crafts and other expressive activities, like dance, music, mime and play-making.

The generally co-educational primary grades, too, have changed greatly from the once ubiquitous stereotype of a basic knowledge and skills factory. This has been especially so with the removal of examinations for progression to secondary education. The three Rs, reading, writing and arithmetic, were probably associated with a fourth R, recording, since 'book work' has long been a fetish of inspectors and a time-consumer for both teachers and students in primary schools. While the emphasis on these four Rs has not disappeared, it is now in better perspective; new emphasis seems to be placed on responsibility and research.

New methods and broader studies   Perhaps the first breath of new methodological techniques came with experiments in teaching social studies by way of so-called 'projects' and 'central themes', instead of separate lessons in history, geography, civics and morals, while much more recently natural science has been infused with the elements of general science knowledge, admittedly at an elementary level. There is now much heavier emphasis on active methods of learning, and much less on note-taking, drill methods and rote memorisation. Another development, it would seem, is the transformation of art lessons from directed, skill-forming exercises to the wide use of a variety of media, with excellent and attractive results. The teaching of music has also been transformed; whereas once emphasis was on singing skills (two- and four-part singing being common) and on classical folk songs (usually originating from the United Kingdom), the emphasis now is increasingly on modern, more meaningful songs and tunes, and especially on the learning of various musical instruments. Music-making has come into its own.

Libraries of pleasing dimensions with well-stocked shelves are finding their way into primary schools and, indeed, the amount and variety of reading material for children has shown tremendous improvement over the past two decades. This trend has been assisted by an upsurge in the production of Australian fiction for young people, and a generally richer supply by publishers of interesting and attractive works of non-fiction. State education departments still produce school papers or magazines for the primary grade child, and some also provide textbooks, while in other states a much wider range of texts and reference books available commercially assist teaching, especially of mathematics, social studies, and English language and literature. Polished verse-speaking choirs are probably not as common today as was once the case, but a wider variety of poetry is introduced to primary girls and boys, and there is a pleasing emphasis on creative poetry and prose writing. Drama and play-making are encouraged, but the results depend very largely on the skills of individual teachers and the standard of production varies remarkably from school to school. As has been stressed previously, emphasis has been placed on the continuous review of sections of the curriculum and, while courses of study are devised by representative committees managed by central authority, the syllabuses (as they are usually called) are generally less prescriptive and give much more freedom to the individual school and teacher than hitherto. The exception is probably mathematics, but teachers have considerable freedom otherwise, as, for example, in the pursuit of physical education, games and organised sport, to which considerable time in the school week is usually given. In a small number of schools, some experimentation with teaching a foreign language in the last primary school year has taken place. In general, then, it can be said that the primary school of today is a far happier centre for learning, and teaching encompasses a broader spectrum of skills and knowledge than the basic literacy school of the nineteenth century from which it grew.

School organisation   The organisation of schools varies. In some, students are streamed according to ability, as estimated by teachers or as measured by standardised achievement tests, or intelligence testing. Increasingly, however, teachers themselves are questioning the wisdom of early ability grouping and, where more than a single class is provided for the grade, 'parallel' classes, each encompassing the whole range of ability, are sometimes favoured. The thoughtful primary teacher sees his (or more frequently these days, her) group as a social community, or family, and the classroom atmosphere is friendly and relatively happy and secure. Specialist teachers are rare, except perhaps for some crafts or where a particular member of the school staff has special expertise. Corporal punishment, once the bane of the child's life, is officially frowned upon; the widespread use of modern methods minimises the need for it, and physical chastisement is strictly controlled.

The increasing informality of the school is assisted by various schemes for ungrading classes and team-teaching experiments, which have met with varying degrees of success. Some schools based on the principles of open planning are making their appearance, especially in South Australia and the Australian Capital Territory. For a number of years individual 'learning laboratories' (self-administering and self-corrective materials) have been in use, and these have assisted to a considerable extent in catering for individual rates of learning. Formal examinations once or twice per year now tend to be less prominent, but regular class testing on a weekly or monthly basis is still emphasised, and much use is made of ACER's basic skills tests (see p 44) which are administered in about September of each year and cover a wide range of skills appropriate to the primary school. Unfortunately, despite the fact that many primary teachers have themselves had experience of multiple group teaching in one-teacher school situations, deliberate provision within a primary class to meet the needs of the individual or of a small group is frequently far from ideal. On the credit side, however, one can point to the use of movable furniture, the use of display boards for children's own work, the employment of sound films and film strips, and the reception of television and radio lessons broadcast by the Australian Broadcasting Commission.

Thus the curriculum and methods of the modern Australian primary school provide, in the best institutions, an air of excitement and busy activity, and promote an enthusiasm for learning. Despite the emphasis on creative activities and group projects, the better primary teacher ensures that the basic skills which parents still consider are most important are well catered for. It is rare to find extreme free methods in use; it is much more common, unfortunately, to find mediocre approaches still in fashion. To this statement, largely applicable to government schools, one must add that independent preparatory schools which supply students to non-government secondary schools are also changing, but remain stricter in their discipline and more traditional in their methods; that Catholic primary schools are gradually becoming far more adventurous and experimental, and are moving rapidly to co-education; and that there are now appearing (with the resurgence of state aid) a few experimental, progressive, independent primary schools in some of the larger cities. With the heavy national emphasis on secondary and tertiary education expansion in recent years, the primary school has tended to be somewhat neglected, but the current situation augurs well for the future, and for a stimulating environment for the next stage of growth in primary school enrolments, expected before 1980.[2]

PROVISION FOR ISOLATED STUDENTS

It has long been official policy in Australia to try to ensure as good an education for children in isolated rural areas as for city children, an attitude no doubt reflecting Australian egalitarianism. An outback station can be almost as isolated from its neighbour as from the coastal city, since some stations are as large as an English county. The vast distances, and lack of communications and transportation have long posed serious problems, but the educational barrier thereby created has not proved insurmountable.

Correspondence schools   In the present century the first successful move to overcome the problems of isolation was the opening of correspondence schools, or 'schools in the mailbox'. The first began in 1916 and subsequently the scheme has been adopted by most authorities. Although the correspondence school scheme does not allow for the social interaction of children in a classroom, as far as possible other aspects of education are competently catered for by the written word, the printed page and the postman. Parental help and supervision are essential, and the standard reached by many correspondence pupils in penmanship, written expression and mathematics has been high indeed. Teachers, employed by a state education department and located in a capital city, send lessons to, and correct exercises from, children in distant locations, children too ill to attend a normal school, those temporarily overseas, prisoners, and young people taking secondary courses in schools where the number of enrolments is small and the range of subjects limited. Reference libraries are provided for those enrolled.

Schools of the air   A relatively recent innovation which greatly helps correspondence education is the School of the Air, the first of which commenced operations in 1951. There are now a dozen of these schools conducted with the assistance of the Royal Flying Doctor Service radio network. Most of the isolated stations in outback Australia have radio transceivers to contact their nearest Flying Doctor base. Between certain hours the communication system thus provided gives two-way communication for teacher and pupils, so that in effect the teacher at base has a class of pupils scattered over thousands of square miles, and yet indulging in most of the activities found in a normal school classroom. This scheme provides many of the activities which correspondence tuition by itself cannot do, and is a valuable adjunct to that instruction. For example, the School of the Air can, and does, provide singing, assemblies, even drama and the sharing of the news.

The small band of teachers who undertake this work rarely see their pupils, but regularly hear them. The exception is when a pupil and his family 'come to town', perhaps for supplies, business reasons, or for medical treatment which necessitates a hospital visit. Some of the schools of the air arrange annual gatherings for staff and pupils, as meetings cannot be frequent when travel often involves distances of up to 1,000 miles.

The number of primary-age children enrolled in correspondence schools is declining steadily, but secondary enrolments are variable. The reasons for this trend include the generally greater affluence (enabling children to be sent to boarding schools, or to live in hostels in the larger country or provincial centres), fewer people living in the outback, the inability of some smaller government secondary schools in provincial centres to provide a wide range of electives, and a trend towards better and cheaper transport to school. In particular, the provision of bus transport to schools—except in the far outback—has been greatly extended and much of the cost is borne by governments. There are instances of buses travelling 50–60 miles each day in each direction. This is said to be more economical than correspondence or small school operation, although the strain on the children who have to make such long daily trips is undeniable. In New South Wales alone, the cost of meeting travelling expenses for school students rose from a little more than $2\frac{1}{2}$ million dollars in 1960 to some $9\frac{1}{2}$ million ten years later. The rise in Victoria, a more compact state of lesser distances, has been almost as great. Much of this money supports rural school bus transportation.

Small, one-teacher rural schools A trend associated with the increased tendency to 'bus' country children to school and the decline in correspondence school enrolments is the closure of small schools. Once a distinctive feature of Australian educational systems, the one-teacher school—catering perhaps for two dozen children aged from five years to twelve or fourteen—is rapidly disappearing in many country areas. The problem of providing teachers skilled in multiple-grade teaching is thereby solved, and it is considered more economical to transport children to a central and larger school, as well as educationally more beneficial. There are, however, many small communities that mourn the passing of their 'school', a one-room building with shelter and out-houses, perhaps with eucalyptus or peppercorn trees in the playground, and often not another structure in sight. Sometimes these isolated schools have residences attached for the teacher and his family, but it is a lonely life and the teacher is dependent for intellectual stimulation on the rare visit from the district inspector or the annual 'small schools conference' in the nearest large town.

SECONDARY SCHOOLS

It is almost impossible to generalise satisfactorily about the structure of secondary education in Australia, except to state that it is five to six years in length, and is divided formally or informally by examination barrier or assessment stage into a larger section of junior secondary education and a smaller section, the senior school, distinctly oriented to meeting entrance requirements for the various forms of higher education. What will be done here, by way of explanation, is to refer the reader to Fig 4, which gives a structural outline for each state and to offer brief comments on all state systems with rather more discussion of one or two.[3]

The state secondary school systems   Since 1962 New South Wales has had a six-year secondary pattern, the first four leading to the award of a School Certificate (originally a fully external examination, but now comprising 75 per cent assessment by the school), and two further years leading to the Higher School Certificate, an external examination. Each of these examinations can be taken at three levels, and it is possible to attain a certificate at different levels in each subject taken. For example, a fairly adept student may obtain her School Certificate with 'advanced' level passes in English and mathematics, 'credit' level passes in French and home economics, 'ordinary' passes in science and history, and a 'modified' pass in, say, art. ('Credit' passes are awarded for good performance at 'ordinary' level.) Such a spread

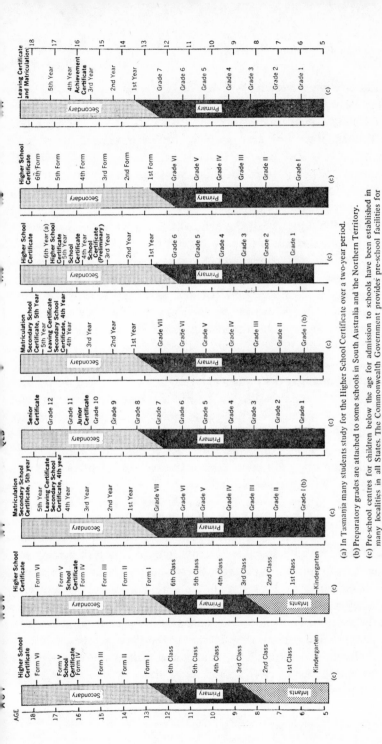

Fig 4 Grades in Australian schools. The grade terminology follows, as nearly as possible, that used in government primary and high schools in each state in 1972. It is not necessarily used in all types of schools. The grades have been written in to agree with the age-scale shown on the diagram, in order to indicate differences in age-grade patterns between states

(a) In Tasmania many students study for the Higher School Certificate over a two-year period.

(b) Preparatory grades are attached to some schools in South Australia and the Northern Territory.

(c) Pre-school centres for children below the age for admission to schools have been established in many localities in all States. The Commonwealth Government provides pre-school facilities for children in the A.C.T. and N.T.

of ability is not very likely, but courses are available for the first four years at the three (really four) levels in most subjects. A core of English, mathematics, science, and a social science must be taken, together with certain attendance requirements in art and craft, music and physical education. The 'modified' level is interesting, being introduced for young people of below average ability, so that it is possible for a very large percentage of the school population to obtain the School Certificate.

After the fourth year, the nature of the curriculum changes in one principal respect: the standard of work required of students becomes, abruptly and distinctly, far more difficult and demanding. Three levels are available—first, second and third—signifying an order of difficulty. First-level courses are very demanding indeed, so that second-level offerings are far more popular. Passes in five subjects at second level usually result in university matriculation. During the School Certificate year the candidate is usually about sixteen (that is, one year beyond the age at which he can generally, if he wishes, legally leave school) and may sit for the Commonwealth Secondary Scholarship Examination conducted on an Australia-wide basis by means of special ACER-devised papers. The winning of a Commonwealth Secondary Scholarship, presently not subject to a means test, results in a living allowance for the last two school years of about sixty dollars per term, a textbook allowance and certain other payments. The test is a difficult one, and is designed to select those with intellectual ability of a considerable order.

The additional year introduced to New South Wales schools was designed to provide an 'orientation' first form in order that the student might sample what the secondary school has to offer. A selection of two electives (in addition to the core subjects already mentioned) takes place at the end of the first form, and after many students have had some general instruction in foreign languages. On the first introduction of the elective scheme, it was possible in many schools for students to make a very wide selection and many elective classes were quite small, but staffing difficulties have been responsible for some diminution in the range. Nevertheless, the present arrangements provide a far more flexible system of choice for secondary subjects and levels than was the case prior to 1962.

In addition to the more comprehensive high schools in New South Wales, there are a few special schools. A small number of selective high schools, left-overs from the days of selection for secondary school prior to 1962, remain in Sydney largely because of the vested interests of alumni, but their degree of selectivity (that is, the minimum intelligence quotient for entry) is declining with the establishment of nearby comprehensive high schools which have seriously eroded their feeder areas. The Conservatorium High School (also in Sydney) provides for young people who show special ability in music but, in addition to musical training, a normal secondary course is followed to Higher School Certificate level. There are also four agricultural high schools, three of which provide boarding facilities. Again, in addition to the special emphasis on agriculture, a normal secondary school course is provided. In areas of small or scattered population there are central schools, which provide both primary and secondary education where an attendance of at least twenty secondary students can be maintained.

The subjects available at high school are interesting. In addition to the usual offerings, it is possible to study for the School Certificate subjects like Asian social studies, Bahasa Indonesia, Dutch, Japanese, Russian, bookcrafts and leathercrafts, ceramics, graphic art and bookbinding, weaving, and sheep husbandry and wool science—although not all of these are available at all levels. The wide range is indicative of two trends, namely, the growing bias towards Asian studies, and of better provision for the non-academic student. To qualify for the award of the School Certificate, a candidate must be examined in at least five subjects and pass in at least four at one sitting.

The educational ladder in Victoria differs from more usual Australian practice in a number of ways. There is, on entry to

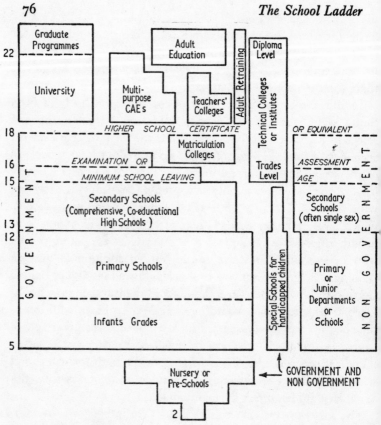

Fig 5   The Australian educational ladder, a generalised representation indicating neither actual proportions of students at various levels nor practices necessarily followed in every state or territory. For likely grade applications and a number of state variations refer to text and/or figure 4

secondary school, a variety of pathways. Victorian high schools have shown very rapid growth in the post-war period, but higher elementary and central schools still exist in places. Victoria also has junior technical schools at the early adolescent stage, together with some girls' secondary schools.

Although the range of secondary schools in Victoria might suggest a rigid degree of selection and direction of secondary students, this is not the case. There is a great deal in common

between the high schools (by far the most common type) and
technical schools in aims, content and curricula. Placing is
dependent on parental wishes. High schools enjoy an increased
amount of freedom in arranging their educational programmes,
and there are many variations to 'normal' procedure and many
experiments in operation, especially now that the burden of
external examinations has been largely removed from the
secondary course. Integrated general studies courses are spoken
of very highly, co-education is increasingly frequent, and the
tendency to delay specialisation is being extended. From 1973
the only external examination will be the Higher School Certificate at the conclusion of the sixth year. This is conducted by the
Victorian Universities and Schools Examination Board. There
is also a Technical Leaving Examination (externally in the fifth
year) for boys and girls taking technical rather than general
courses, and a modified industrial course for boys who intend to
leave school at fifteen years. As elsewhere in Australia, in smaller
country centres there are some primary schools offering some
secondary instruction: these are known as higher elementary,
central, group or consolidated schools.

A development of some interest in Victorian secondary education has been the opening, as part of the government system, of
street corner or church-hall schools (as, for example, the Swinburne Community School). This scheme offers more mobility to
the student and, it is hoped, will encourage more self-reliance
and responsibility. There seems to be more encouragement for
such innovatory practices today than appeared to be given by
state authorities in the early sixties when, for example, experiments were made with a core of social problems curriculum at
the Henry Lawson High School in Grenfell, a central-west town
of New South Wales.

The extent of non-government secondary education in Victoria is important. In Melbourne especially there are numerous
grammar schools, usually under the auspices of religious denominations or having a close connection with them; these are heavily

supported by Melbournians and enjoy a high status, even though there are differences between them, and between them and state schools, making for a distinct pecking order in secondary education.

Five years of secondary education are offered in Western Australia. Although students may leave school at the end of the year in which they turn fifteen, about 90 per cent of students complete three years of secondary education and about 25 per cent complete the full five-year course. The types of schools include senior high schools (leading to the Leaving Certificate after five years' attendance), high schools (three-year courses) and junior high schools (like central schools). There are also two agricultural junior high schools, a senior agricultural high school, Perth Modern Senior High School which caters additionally for the talented in music, and another for art. Assessment is used for the Achievement Certificate (obtained after three secondary years) although some external control of standards is maintained by the Board of Secondary Education. The curriculum is quite wide and subjects are offered at various levels.

The situation in Queensland, long regarded by southerners as the most conservative state educationally, is interesting. Five years of secondary education (instead of four) are now provided in grades 8–12, which are normally entered in the year a student turns thirteen. High schools, now existing in much greater numbers, provide for a wide range of abilities and interests, but as elsewhere a number of primary schools have secondary 'tops' in centres of smaller population, and some students are catered for by the Secondary Correspondence School. The basic principles followed in Queensland's high schools are those of co-education and comprehensive organisation, with a first year (Grade 8) not specialised, that is, with a balanced core course provided, similar to that in New South Wales, but with foreign languages offered. Electives are chosen at the commencement of Grade 9 and syllabuses in the senior years are arranged in semester units. As in most other states, the curriculum is controlled by a statutory board— in Queensland's case the Board of Secondary School Studies.

However, subjects may, with approval, be offered by a school on its own initiative. The Board also makes arrangements for the assessment of students for the award of its certificates. There has been a marked change from external examinations to moderated school assessment in Queensland in recent years.

The position in South Australia is still quite complex, despite remarks made elsewhere (see Chapter 6) about the progressive nature of much of South Australian educational arrangements. There are three kinds of government secondary schools, high, technical and area schools, and courses are still denoted by the term 'tracks'. However, there is a very heavy swing away from formal, external examinations to assessments and the moderation of internal examinations.

Tasmania has had a long history of experiment with different forms of secondary education, what with its area schools of the 1930s, a tripartite secondary experiment after World War II, and, since the abolition of the Classification Test in 1962, its comprehensive and non-selective high schools. The most interesting and recent innovation, however, has been the establishment of matriculation colleges and centres. There are three matriculation colleges, two in Hobart (the capital) and one in Launceston (Tasmania's second major city), which enrol fifth- and sixth-year students studying for the Tasmanian Higher School Certificate, while matriculation centres are attached to two other high schools at Devonport and Burnie. Additional matriculation colleges are planned, and it will be interesting to observe the extent to which other states follow Tasmania's lead.

In addition to the high schools, Tasmania has district schools somewhat like central schools in other states, and providing both primary and secondary schooling. Area schools still exist in rural districts and, in general, offer three-year secondary courses leading to the School Certificate Preliminary Award, but in an increasing number of districts the course is being extended to four years. A few primary schools in really isolated rural areas have small secondary groups and, as in other states, a correspondence school operates as well. The School Certificate at the end of the fourth secondary year is awarded after assessment procedures, but the Higher School Certificate is taken as an external examination.

The population of the Northern Territory is small and the Territory returns only one of the one hundred and twenty-five members of the Federal House of Representatives. There are two government high schools in Darwin (with a third under construction) and one in Alice Springs. In addition, secondary as well as primary education is provided in four other government schools in various parts of the Territory and at two non-government schools in Darwin. Because of existing arrangements with South Australia (whose staff are now being withdrawn) students follow the South Australian curriculum and take South Australian examinations.

Non-government secondary schools   In view of the fact that non-government schools exist in their greatest numbers at secondary level, a separate word about them seems in order. While some non-government schools may be called high schools and offer much the same secular curriculum as government schools, it is much more common for them to be styled grammar schools, colleges, or given a religious name, either that of a saint or the name of the religious order conducting the establishment. Few have been co-educational, but there is an increasing tendency for co-educational classes to exist, especially at senior level, or for two schools of the same religious denomination to be merged or co-operate closely in some appropriate way, usually for economic, rather than educational, reasons. Except where demand is heavy, there is usually no entrance test, although preference is given in most cases to the children of former students or to children of the denomination which manages the school. The main deviation of the school curriculum is in the teaching of religious knowledge and dogma, and its assessment as for a secular course or subject. A morning assembly of a religious character and religious exercises are usual. There is often a heavy emphasis on organised team sport, although more unusual and individual sporting activities are now being encouraged. Perhaps the best known experiment in Australian non-government schools is 'Timbertops' school, run by Geelong Grammar School, where students in a junior secondary grade spend a year in bush and mountain surroundings away from the main school site. In the very best non-government schools, a wide range of cultural, social and sporting activities is to be found; of course, the boarding school nature of many establishments assists this.

Reference has already been made to the registration of teachers in non-government schools. Since 1932, for example, the Teachers and Schools Registration Board in Tasmania has had the responsibility of registering non-government schools and all teachers working in those schools in that state. The Board lays down minimum requirements for school registration and teacher qualifications; once a school is registered it is not normally inspected, although the Board legally is empowered to do so. The Tasmanian Education Department may inspect schools, but only for the purpose of enforcing compulsory school attendance; deparmental inspectors do visit some such schools by invitation and, no doubt, to the mutual benefit and illumination of both the inspecting officers and the school. In Victoria, the corresponding authority is the Council of Public Education and the arrangements which exist are similar to those of Tasmania.

The recruitment of staff for a non-government school is generally the responsibility of the head, although, in the case of Catholic schools, there is an increasing tendency for the diocesan Catholic education office to act as a recruiting agency. In addition there are a number of commercial agencies which assist independent schools; the final decision on accepting an applicant for a post, however, remains the head's responsibility. The position in government schools is far different: staffing appointments are centralised at 'head office' or area office, since promotion is based on a teacher's seniority in a state-wide teaching service. It is usual for a state education department to pay allowances to

F

teachers-in-training so that, when their preparation is complete, they must accept appointment to any school and serve their state for a number of years.

Influences on the secondary school   In Australia there is a definite trend towards abandoning the traditional external examination. The university as an institution has tended to dominate secondary school curricula, teaching methods and attitudes by virtue of its entrance requirements. Each state developed its own leaving or matriculation examination, but the latest tendency is for universities to experiment with new forms of assessment, including the acceptance of the school principal's recommendation.[4] Accrediting long ago constituted an early form of university entrance in some circumstances in Victoria. Currently, the situation could be said to be one of flux.

Considerable attention has been paid in Australian schools to more frequent curriculum revision. The secondary school, long the preserve of 'chalk and talk', is feeling the influence of this movement, and of interest in more active ways of learning. For example, secondary English courses are less prescriptive, more directed towards creative activities like poetry and play-writing, film scripting and production, and the careful relation of texts read to the students' own writing in a creative and imaginative way. Possibly 'flexibility' is the best description of the new approach, and it demands a changed attitude on the part of the teacher. The development of the student's critical powers is regarded as highly important, and it is thought that this may be attained through the more careful relation of literary material to his own interests and experience of life. Among the techniques being used are theme approaches, the discussion of current magazines and controversial books, and encouraging the expression of personal reactions and opinions. Skill development is stressed, perhaps even at the price of subject matter. These trends are, of course, to be expected, since the high school is no longer merely for an academic élite, but for the general education of all adolescents.

Greatly increased secondary enrolments have resulted in the building of many new secondary schools, complete with facilities to encourage the use of new teaching methods. Art and craft spaces, gymnasiums, drama workshops and special music rooms, well-equipped science laboratories and demonstration rooms, libraries complete with study carrels and group discussion rooms, and language laboratories are now commonplace in many centres.

Australian society has always been less ruled by concepts of class and tradition than many countries are, and has exhibited a pragmatic approach to its problems. This may be a reason why little has been written concerning the philosophy of Australian education. Probably the most certain fact about the educational philosophy held is that, in a country with a great middle stratum of society the schools mirror, in general, middle-class mores. This would certainly be true of the government schools and, since independent schools follow much the same secular curricula as the government schools, it is obvious that middle-class values permeate the non-government sector too, as well as upper strata outlooks. Perhaps the extent to which middle-class attitudes are operative in the society is reflected in the widespread opposition to socially select schools with an independent base, and on the other hand the neglect of education in certain depressed areas. Examples would be schools catering largely for migrant populations and aborigines.

A further influence on the outlook of the school is the fact of six centralised state systems of education; this imposes a considerable degree of intra- and inter-state uniformity, which some critics regard as oppressive, but which at the same time encourages a spread of equality of educational opportunity that might otherwise be impossible. And it is the belief in equality of opportunity which runs through the whole of the government school systems. Basically, it seems to be the case that the opportunity which the states try to provide is designed so that the individual has the best possible opportunity (that is, a fair chance) to develop his or her own potential, or to 'get on' in life.

4

Universities and Colleges

THE UNIVERSITIES

In general, courses offered by Australian universities are full-time day courses normally taking three to six years for completion (for instance, an arts course is three years, medicine six years). Provision is made for part-time, including evening, study for certain subjects, especially where laboratory attendance is not required. A few universities have well-established systems of external studies, as for example in arts, education and economics. All Australian universities make provision for postgraduate studies and research.

Enrolments and offerings Symptomatic of the heavily increased numbers clamouring for university education (there were 28,000 university students in 1953, whereas 147,700 are expected in 1975), university enrolments are quite heavily skewed towards arts faculties (28 per cent) with about 20 per cent in science, 12 per cent in medicine, 10 per cent in engineering and 8 per cent in economics.[1] In each case, there is a recognised number of extremely popular subjects: English, history, psychology and sociology in arts, economics and accounting in economics faculties, mathematics, geology, chemistry and physics in science, for example.[2] However, the range of subjects offered at universities is wide, although some universities are recognised centres for certain subjects. Examples of specialism include veterinary science at Sydney, Asian languages at Melbourne and the Australian National University, Canberra, technical subjects at the

University of New South Wales and rural science at the University of New England.

Australian universities tend to have a larger number of faculties than those in the United Kingdom:[3] Sydney, Melbourne, Queensland and Adelaide all have more than ten faculties and their enrolments are very large, too, usually in excess of most British institutions. On the other hand, they are considerably smaller than many of their American counterparts. Because of the absence until recently of a variety of tertiary institutions, there is a heavy emphasis on professional education at the Australian university: a count shows that the fifteen universities had 656 subjects in their calendars, and of these 335 are distinctly professional, 116 in the category of pure science and 205 in the area of the humanities.[4]

Concern over teaching methods   Teaching methods at Australian universities have often been typified as traditional, and complaints about the quality of teaching have been increasingly vocal. However, there is now some evidence to suggest that innovations in, and concern about, tertiary-level teaching are increasing within the institutions themselves. Concerned about the predominance of the lecture method, the comparative dearth of tutorial and seminar, and with the little use made of modern media for audiovisual instruction, the Australian Vice-Chancellors' Committee in 1964–5 conducted a survey of teaching methods in the universities. The resultant findings favoured taking into greater account the teaching ability of applicants for staff appointments, training courses for new lecturers, emphasis on smaller class groups, better library facilities, and the need for follow-up studies to assess the impact of courses on students.[5]

Staff-student relations in the teaching-learning process have been of particular concern. Research evidence shows that a greater proportion of students prefer tutorials and small group meetings. The student representative councils at most universities and the Australian Union of Students have been very critical about the quality of university teaching, and have appointed

education research officers in an attempt to do something about
the problem. Monash University's education diploma course[6]
and that of the University of New England (both designed to
cater for the teacher interested or involved in tertiary teaching),
as well as the establishment of higher education research units,
show that the universities are not content to leave the problem
to student organisations.

Yet it is not merely a question of improving teaching methods
for the sake of doing so. The high drop-out rate and the low
percentages of students graduating in minimum course time have
long been causes for concern. The beginning of continuous assessment, rather than the trauma of the annual examination, is one
overdue response to this problem; another is experimentation
with different types of examination (objective testing is more in
favour in some subject areas). In the medical teaching field, the
Association of University Clinical Professors of Australia has
decided to establish a national bank of multiple choice questions
from which examiners can draw.[7] Programmed instruction and
teaching by closed-circuit television have been tried, usually in
response to huge groups enrolled in the larger universities in
basic courses. In summary, then, it may be said that in the last
decade staff, students, taxpayers and the vice-chancellors themselves have exhibited increasing concern for the effectiveness of
university instruction. There is more than a suspicion that this
interest has been accelerated by the advent of colleges of advanced
education, the very existence of which provides something of a
challenge to the universities. Certainly, an increased amount of
research is being conducted in the area of teaching effectiveness
and student assessment.

Graduate study and research   Several other features of
Australian universities are of interest. Graduate programmes have
expanded—doctoral programmes in particular—especially in the
natural sciences and in certain social sciences, to the partial
eclipse of the popularity of masters' degrees attained by thesis.
On the other hand an upsurge in masters' degrees by course work

is taking place. Postgraduate expansion reflects the growing concentration of interest by university staff in research projects. Indeed, the proliferation of research and the rising requests for research funds by individual university staff members and research teams have led to attempts to rationalise research at this level. An early impetus to research in scientific fields was made by the work of the Commonwealth Scientific and Industrial Research Organisation, sponsored by the Commonwealth government. Both pure and applied research have been greatly encouraged by CSIRO.

Student unrest   In keeping with trends overseas, an amount of student unrest has manifested itself in the universities. Perhaps it would not be an unfair generalisation to say that during the fifties the Australian campuses were extremely quiet, and a generally held theory was that, with more students taking university courses through the Commonwealth Scholarship Scheme or teacher scholarships, there was an emphasis on gaining qualifications. However, the percentage of assisted students has, since that era, increased further, and the disturbances of the late sixties and early seventies indicate that sponsorship is hardly enough to turn students away from protesting against what they see as social and political injustices. Vietnam, conscription and aboriginal rights seem to have stirred the student conscience most, especially in the larger centres like Sydney, Brisbane and Melbourne. Although student demonstration on these and like issues has not been on the same scale as disturbances in other countries, it has no doubt affected community attitudes, either positively in hardening opinion on matters like conscription, or negatively in reinforcing community doubts about the role of universities in the society. Traditionally, Australians appear to have had little enough trust in the highly educated. Students have also demanded participation in university government, and to an extent concessions in this direction have been made, but so far without fundamental alteration to the balance of university power. Students have also requested courses of their own choosing to count towards degrees, but these moves have been relatively muted. Finally, there has been a change in student attitude towards residence. At New England University which, for internal students, is largely residential, a trend towards town and apartment living, and grouping together in communes, has made the maintenance of full student college accommodation very difficult. Significantly perhaps, that university with seven large residential colleges is not planning any more, a decision having been made to experiment with apartment residence in the future.

The greatly increased student numbers and the heavy demand for places suggest that the university, as an institution, is largely seen in Australian eyes as a prime vehicle of educational opportunity. In its percentage of the population accorded entry, the Australian university stands somewhere between English and American practice, for it is neither as selective as the English university, nor draws upon so large a percentage of high school graduates as its USA counterpart. The establishment of colleges of advanced education reflects a concern, among government ranks, that the percentage aspiring to university education has been too high, and that failure rates have been too acute. In other words, it has been felt that many entering universities would be better placed in other more practical institutions.

Finance and government   With the vast increase in spending on universities both by the states and the Commonwealth government, the matter of the efficiency of universities has been taken in hand and there is now less autonomy for universities than was once the case. They are told what to do and when, and how much it may cost. Indeed, the extent of control by the Australian Universities Commission is such that the much-vaunted academic autonomy of the universities now seems to be in a parlous state.

The Australian Universities Commission arranges finance for the universities on a triennial basis, which allows an amount of forward planning. Thus universities have to submit their plans well in advance, both for buildings and organisational changes, and these are carefully scrutinised. For example, the AUC would be particularly interested were a university, organised on a traditional faculty basis, to propose organisation into rather smaller units or 'schools', which indeed some universities have done. Among other changes which have enjoyed rising popularity are semesters instead of the traditional three university terms per year. Changes also include some modification of academic government within the universities, including the suggested disappearance of the professorial board, which is attacked on the grounds that it represents a professorial oligarchy and gives insufficient voice in academic affairs to other and lesser members of staff.

Australian universities are staffed very much on the British pattern of professor, reader or associate professor, senior lecturer and lecturer (positions with tenure), senior tutor and tutor, and research assistant. Large departments have more than one professor. During the period of most rapid expansion of the universities, there were distinct problems of academic recruitment, but the present problem seems to revolve more around the need for junior staff to cope with large classes. These classes are composed of the key feature of most Australian campuses, the commuter student, although many universities do also have residential colleges attached. The universities, in English parlance, are more likely to be typified as redbrick or plateglass—or a combination of both—rather than Oxbridge.

COLLEGES OF ADVANCED EDUCATION

When in 1965 the Federal government accepted the recommendations of the Martin Committee on the establishment of tertiary colleges, Victoria was the first state to move to establish an organisation which could receive and spend Federal funds for this purpose: hence the creation of the Victoria Institute of Colleges and the heavy emphasis in Victoria on advanced education. Subsequently, each other state established a similar organisation although, in the light of different circumstances existing in each state, the method of organisation is slightly different. New South Wales, Queensland and South Australia each have boards of advanced education, Tasmania a council of advanced education, Western Australia a tertiary education commission, while reference has already been made to the Canberra-based Australian Commission on Advanced Education. The latest creation is the Australian Council on Awards in Advanced Education, also located in Canberra, and charged with responsibility for accrediting the degrees and diplomas awarded in the various non-university institutions concerned.

Applied studies and good teaching   Colleges of advanced education offer tertiary courses, designed to provide an even greater vocational emphasis than is the case at the universities. In part, CAEs are being developed from the existing tertiary sections of already established technical institutions and colleges, and in part by means of the establishment of new colleges. There are over forty CAEs. The wide range of courses throughout the six states and in the Australian Capital Territory makes generalisation difficult concerning a specific pattern of courses for which degrees and diplomas are provided; what can be said is that emphasis is on applied rather than on pure studies. Their course offerings include accountancy, architecture, art, applied chemistry building, business management, data processing, engineering, librarianship, mathematics, medical laboratory technology, metallurgy, nutrition, pharmacy, physics and textile sciences. In addition, in some multi-purpose CAEs teacher education courses have been provided, while single-purpose teachers' colleges in New South Wales are now also considered as CAEs. Other specialist institutions have been changed in status to colleges of advanced education: examples include the NSW Conservatorium of Music, agricultural colleges and the National Institute of Dramatic Art.

Colleges of advanced education are seen by the Australian Commission on Advanced Education as quite distinct from universities, their purpose being to 'increase the range of opportunity for tertiary education having a strong emphasis on practical application. . . . The performance of its graduates in industry and society rather than their qualifications will be the criterion by which the community judges the college system'.[8] Thus, the emphasis in the CAEs is definitely centred on good teaching for a first degree or diploma, rather than on research.

Because of their recent introduction and deliberate government policy and financing, CAE enrolments have been growing at a faster rate than university numbers; in 1969 some 32,000 students were enrolled, but by 1975 the figure is expected to reach 81,000.[9] The colleges vary tremendously in size; in 1971 the Royal Melbourne Institute of Technology enrolled nearly 9,000 whereas Victoria's Creswick School of Forestry had only 27 students. In general, part-time and sandwich courses supplement full-time offerings, the academic year is usually about 33 weeks, and industrial experience is required. While the basic essential for Federal money is that a CAE must offer at least a two-year diploma course, which many do, increasingly there is a trend to degree courses, now certified by the Australian Council on Awards in Advanced Education.

The Victoria Institute of Colleges   The Victoria Institute of Colleges is well established. It has an extensive committee system and has endorsed a wide system of diploma and degree awards outside the university orbit. It is far from opposed to part-time work for degrees and has already given favourable consideration to masters' and doctoral degrees. The colleges affiliated with the VIC include a number in Melbourne, all of which, to a greater or less extent, are multi-purpose institutions. The Royal Melbourne Institute of Technology is by far the largest and most wide-ranging in its course offerings. In addition, however, there are a number of specialist colleges affiliated with the VIC (the Victorian School of Speech Science and the Victorian College of Pharmacy, for example) and country colleges located at the provincial centres of Ballarat, Bendigo, Warrnambool, and in Gippsland. The new buildings provided under the aegis of the VIC are impressive: the new library at Swinburne College of Technology and the buildings at Preston in Melbourne are pertinent examples.

NSW pattern   The New South Wales government has established multi-purpose colleges of advanced education incorporating nearby teachers' colleges. Mitchell College is based on the former Bathurst Teachers' College and Riverina CAE is based on the former Wagga Teachers' College. This policy is to be extended by Kingswood College on the western outskirts of Sydney, a rapidly growing residential and industrial area, and incorporating Westmead Teachers' College while a multi-pupose college is to be provided at Lismore, incorporating the recently opened Lismore Teachers' College. At Kingswood, business studies and applied science will be offered in addition to courses in teacher education, while the new offering at Northern Rivers CAE will probably be business studies. Some time ago the NSW College of Occupational Therapy, the School of Physiotherapy, the Speech Therapy Training School and the NSW School of Orthoptics were made CAEs but these, together with the NSW College of Nursing, are to be incorporated in a College of Paramedical Studies, also to be located in Sydney. Thus, in addition to the principle of multi-purpose institutions, there is some evidence of another principle (especially when one considers the huge new NSW Institute of Technology in central Sydney, also under the banner of advanced education), namely that of grouping allied interests in rather centralised locations.

Although it is not possible here to detail all curricular arrangements at colleges of advanced education, it is of interest to mention some of the new CAEs and their course offerings. The NSW Institute of Technology in Sydney became a corporate (that is, independently governed) institution and college of advanced education in July 1971. It provides degree courses in civil, electrical, mechanical, production and structural engineering, as well as in applied chemistry and bio-medical science; it offers diploma courses in architecture, building, quantity surveying, science, information processing, commerce, management, public administration, public relations and medical technology, and extension courses in systems analysis, vacuum technology, environmental pollution studies, instrumental analysis-chemistry, systems engineering, Cobol and Fortran IV programming. In contrast, Mitchell CAE, a country college in the city of Bathurst about 130 miles west of Sydney, and made corporate from January 1971, provides degree courses in accountancy, economics, industrial and commercial management, public administration, industrial mathematics, general mathematics, decentralisation and quantitative management; diploma courses in various teacher education programmes, journalism and public relations; and associate diploma courses in local government administration and applied arts.[10]

Teaching methods   Generalisation is difficult in the case of the teaching methods employed in colleges of advanced education. However, a study by Horne and Wise found that in business studies, more so than the engineering fields, there appeared a tendency towards more formal lectures followed up with tutorials, while in engineering the general approach was a combination of presentation, questions and discussion.[11] Significantly, perhaps, the 1972 report of the Australian Commission on Advanced Education emphasised the need to turn away from the lecture approach, and to make greater use of the tutorial-seminar-project approach.[12] The Commission stressed the need to secure greater student involvement in learning, and argued the case for the greater use of tutors in CAEs.[13] Other clues to the situation are Horne and Wise's comments on the necessity for more use of teaching aids, the existence of high staff loads and a need for discussion on the regular assignments students are generally required to submit.

There is little doubt that the question of upgrading and making more efficient methods of tertiary-level teaching is much the same, whether the institution is a CAE or a university. It would appear that here is a fertile field for research and experiment;

certainly concern has now been expressed at all tertiary institutions over educational techniques and methods of assessment.

TEACHER PREPARATION

The 'usual' pattern   Until very recently the preparation of teachers in Australia followed much the same pattern as in the United Kingdom. The most usual patterns have been two or three years' preparation in a teachers' college (the equivalent of English colleges of education, without necessarily any connections with a university or area training authority), mainly provided for infant, primary and junior secondary teacher trainees, or a three- or four-year university course followed by a further year's course for the diploma in education, principally designed for the preparation of secondary teachers, and taught either by a university or by a college in association with a university. In general, the college course or university plus diploma 'end-on' pattern has been followed by students under scholarship and/or a bond to serve their employer for a given time after graduation and recruited by state departments of education. Admission to college courses is by completing successfully a secondary school course; increasingly, applicants have also matriculated. The scholarship awarded pays course fees and also provides a living allowance, the amount of which varies from state to state and with the age of the student.

Innovations in teacher education   Teachers' college courses generally follow much the same pattern: education, some major studies (and perhaps an elective or optional subject), methods of teaching the subjects of the school curriculum, physical education, art, craft and music. The weekly lecture and demonstration programme is a busy one, and there are usually two or three periods of practice teaching during the year. Some colleges, especially with the extension of courses from two to three years, are experimenting with new forms of curriculum, while others incorporate some university course work. One of the most interesting approaches is that of Armidale Teachers'

College in New South Wales where the curriculum is divided
into core subjects, electives and professional studies. Its core, for
example, includes courses like 'The Legacy of the Western
World', 'Man in a Scientific and Technological World', and
'Australian Society and Culture'. Electives include such diverse
interests as library practice, field studies, theatre, and industrial
arts, in addition to the more usual curricular offerings. An
interesting departure at this institution is that students are not
required to take all teaching methods applicable to the infant and
primary school.

University preparation of teachers is also changing. Much
more interest is being shown in concurrent preparation—that is,
students are being encouraged to take their degree work *together
with* elements of professional preparation over four or five years.
The aim is to allow a longer period of exposure to educational
ideas and methods than is possible in a single year in the 'end-on'
scheme. This arrangement is offered as an alternative at the
University of New England, while at Macquarie, also in New
South Wales, a master-teacher plan operates in conjunction with
the basic degree course. Increasingly, therefore, professional
educators are experimenting with new approaches, in view of
general dissatisfaction with the tried—and not so trusted—
traditional pattern.

Teachers for non-government schools   Another interesting development in teacher education is the changing attitude of
non-government schools to teacher preparation. For many years
Mercer House in Melbourne has offered training to people
desiring to enter independent schools as teachers, but in general
the schools have preferred in-service training for their recruits.
The Teachers' Guild of New South Wales, however, has begun
its own college for pre-and in-service education, while the
Catholic schools, mainly because of the increased need to recruit
lay teachers, have expanded their provision for teacher education
both by means of colleges and by sending recruits to universities.

While the argument over government support for pre-school

education is still not settled, teacher preparation programmes for pre-school teachers have existed for some time. Today, kindergarten teachers' colleges, providing three-year courses, exist in every state except Tasmania where, however, this kind of preparation is available at teachers' colleges at Hobart and Launceston. Seventeen years is the minimum age of entry to these courses, and matriculation standard is generally required.

OTHER TERTIARY COLLEGES

Technical colleges   Traditionally, technical education courses have been offered mainly on a part-time, or 'learn-as-you-earn', basis. More recently, there has been a trend towards more full-time and sandwich-type courses (as in the United Kingdom) and day-release programmes. Courses provided range from diploma (tertiary-level) courses down to apprenticeship (trades-type) courses. The former give advanced training at post-matriculation level in technical subjects like accountancy and art, and are highly regarded by employers. Below this level (often equated or near-equated with university degrees) is a variety of courses for craftsmen, semi-professional workers and apprentices. Correspondence courses are often available, as are refresher courses in certain fields, and matriculation preparation. Practical work usually dominates the methods of teaching in technical courses and counts towards final assessments. Courses range from applied electricity and aircraft engineering to fashion, food, graphic design, textiles and building trades. Courses are also provided in areas such as hospital administration and real estate valuation.

Although some technical subjects are available at secondary school level and, as has been seen, junior technical schools still exist (as do some technical high schools), most specifically technical training takes place in technical colleges entirely supported by government. To supplement this provision, some technical training courses are provided by private industry and other governmental instrumentalities. A definite trend for students to enter technical training at a later age and with higher educational attainments has been observed. In addition, many technical colleges offer leisure-time courses of general public interest, prepare students for public examinations, and offer a variety of correspondence courses.

Most technical college work is therefore under the control of state departments of education, further or technical education. In all states decentralisation of facilities, to provide more adequately for rural youth, is encouraged, either by the regional establishment of technical college facilities or by means of travelling classrooms and workshops, often in co-operation with rail services. Another trend of considerable significance is towards a shortening of the terms and improving the conditions of apprenticeship.

Agricultural colleges   Various external pressures (for example, British entry to the European Common Market, competition from other sources of agricultural and pastoral produce, and the increasingly uneconomic position of smaller holdings) have led to an increased interest in scientific agriculture in Australia. It is true that Australia rides on the sheep's back and has been a prolific supplier of grains to overseas nations, but most land industries have experienced increasing difficulties, not all to be resolved by Federal subsidy or protection. For many years the improvement of agricultural production and marketing was the province of a few university faculties of agriculture and several widely scattered agricultural colleges, usually controlled by state departments of agriculture. The contemporary tendency is for the courses provided at colleges to be upgraded as to entrance requirements and content, for new establishments to be created and for a more scientific approach to be encouraged to the problems of agricultural extension education, farm management and various associated technologies. In New South Wales for many years there were just three agricultural colleges of senior secondary standard, but the trends noted above have been most marked, including course upgrading and the establishment of two addi-

G

tional colleges. As in other states, the trend is towards the incorporation of such colleges as colleges of advanced education. In Queensland, Gatton Agricultural College has become an autonomous institute and there are three- and four-year courses provided, while Victoria has four centres offering courses of differing lengths and standard, including a course at the Royal Melbourne Institute of Technology in farm maintenance and management. Perhaps the most colourful course is at Roseworthy Agricultural College in South Australia; there a two-year diploma course in oenology, available to students of advanced standing, assists the Australian wine industry.

ADULT EDUCATION

Adult education has not thrived in the Australian context, and there is still considerable room for development and improvement in this area. The Workers' Educational Association (WEA) was established in 1913; forerunners included the nineteenth-century mechanics' institutes and schools of arts. Like their predecessors, the WEA and tutorial classes established by some universities have fought an uphill battle. Three universities in New South Wales have departments of 'extension', or adult education, and use various media—radio, discussion groups, source material kits, bulletins—to reach their clientele. In 1966 the Australian Universities Commission recommended withdrawal of Federal funds from university extension work, but happily this was not endorsed by government; the proposal was no doubt symptomatic of some disappointment with existing adult education programmes. The New South Wales Department of Education maintains a number of evening colleges which offer a variety of courses, and these are supported to varying degrees. Perhaps it is significant that these ventures began as 'youth colleges', but were not patronised by young people who had recently left school; it was the middle-aged and elderly who started to patronise them—hence the change in name. The WEA exists in New South Wales and South Australia, while in Victoria the voluntary counterpart is the Adult Education Association of Victoria. The Australian Institute of Management also operates courses for adults, and agricultural extension work is fairly widespread.

The Australian public, on the whole, is more familiar with the work of the Arts Council of Australia whose specific purpose is to encourage music and arts. This is parallelled by the Elizabethan Theatre Trust and a number of other agencies, all of which are assisted financially by government subsidy to a greater or lesser extent. More familiar still is the Australian Broadcasting Commission which maintains the national broadcasting and television services, parallel to commercial stations and networks. The ABC provides many serious programmes of high artistic or intellectual quality but, with listener ratings in mind, also has to provide much light entertainment. Public library services, art galleries and museums also play a role in adult education.

When Australia's progress in embracing adult education programmes of various kinds is assessed, the position is somewhat disappointing. Only in 1972 was the first move for retraining adults made by government, but there is—by the general public —as yet insufficient appreciation of either the need for retraining in a rapidly growing, complex technological society, or of the general need for continuing education in adult life. It would be hard for a dedicated adult educator not to feel that Australians prefer their beer and poker machines, and exhibit a philistine-like outlook to educational problems, but he should have hopes for the emergence of more public pressure for adult education in the future.

5
State and Commonwealth

As we have seen, education is the responsibility of the six states, except for Commonwealth territories where financial support is a Federal matter. During the past quarter-century, increasing school population and a growing community appreciation of the value of education have resulted in heavy increases in financial commitment to education by all authorities, and in the drawing of the Commonwealth into many aspects of financing educational institutions in the states. Although most reaction to the situation has been on the basis of consumer demand and community need, there is an increasing tendency to view educational expenditure as an economic investment, particularly by the Federal government. As in other countries faced with similar problems, the main constraint on the growing educational budgets has been monetary resources; a problem of special significance to Australia, however, has been the balance of financial power between the states and the Commonwealth.

THE BALANCE OF FINANCIAL POWER

Particular problems associated with financing education have included the need to provide many more school buildings, more teachers, the development of courses in science and technology, and the need to expand the universities. In 1958 the percentage of the gross national product expended on education was estimated at 2·9 per cent (compared with 4·5 per cent in USA and 3·7 per cent in Canada and England). Although low by international standards, the percentage of GNP spent on education has risen since that date: in 1965–6 it was little more than 4 per cent and is now rather nearer 5 per cent.[1]

The Commonwealth enters the educational field The Commonwealth government entered the educational field in two main ways. First, it gained constitutional power to make awards to students. This resulted in Commonwealth University and Postgraduate Scholarships, and later in awards for students in senior secondary classes. During the fifties and sixties, the number and extent of these awards gradually increased; for those successful in the intense competition, the remuneration is high and generous. Second, the desperate position of the universities in 1950 elicited some Commonwealth government assistance, and this was supplemented on a very generous scale following the Murray Report of 1957 and the Martin Report of 1964. Generally, the position is that the Federal government makes financial grants to the states for their universities on the basis of matching grants of $1 Commonwealth for every $1.85 of state funds for recurrent expenditure, and $1 for $1 in the case of capital expenditure. Following the Murray Report's recommendations, as we have seen, an Australian Universities Commission was established to advise the Commonwealth government on these grants, and to supervise (in a manner analogous to the English University Grants Committee) development in university education. In general, this arrangement has been very successful, not only in the case of existing universities, but also in the establishment and growth of new institutions.

Following the recommendations of the Martin Committee in 1964 the Commonwealth also entered a new field of tertiary education—that of colleges of advanced education. In this case establishment grants were followed by the same formula for recurrent and capital expenditure, again on a generous scale; the development of a system of Commonwealth-wide CAEs but under *state* auspices (with the Canberra CAE alone completely financed by the Commonwealth) has been rapid, indeed spectacular. An additional estimate of Federal commitment to educa-

tional expenditure may be gained from noting the introduction
of annual per capita grants to independent schools, assistance
with building (for example, new science accommodation and
library facilities) and the extension of these provisions to new
state schools. Thus, these grants and the provision of scholarship
allowances have assisted the growth of secondary education
to a marked extent. They also indicate how rapidly the
Commonwealth has become involved in supplementing state
finances.

Problems of financing   All these contributions have been
extremely welcome. Many Catholic schools have been in desperate plights for added financial help, but even with the closure
of some small Catholic schools at the secondary level, added aid
is still sought. Although criticism is levelled at the large sums
contributed to wealthy independent (usually non-Catholic)
schools and the prestige buildings many erect with the assistance
provided, it must be remembered that enrolments in these schools
have often risen quite markedly in two decades and that, in
addition, many independent schools are not really wealthy, well
endowed, or charging near-exorbitant feees. In the latter case,
Federal funds, now to an extent supplemented by additional per
capita aid from state governments, have contributed to their sur-
vival in a period of intense inflation. In the instance of some rural
schools in this category, the funding has been a life-line and,
even allowing for this help, some are still in relatively severe
difficulty. Yet Federal funding has not altogether been without
its problems: the states, for example, wishing to accept matched
grants for universities and CAEs, have often been hard put to it
to find the funds necessary to attract the maximum Commonwealth grant. The severe strain put on their distinctly limited
resources has endangered state support for other areas of education, and continues to do so. State difficulties, and criticism of
the extent and method of Commonwealth aid, keep alive a debate
on the mode of national financing of education. This is the more
so since the problem of financing education lies mainly in the

division of financial powers and responsibilities between the Commonwealth and the states where the Commonwealth has the major taxing and loan-raising power.

There are other problems, some not publicised as much as the Commonwealth-state difficulties. One of these is the high cost of providing science and technologically based education as compared with the teaching of the humanities; another is the distribution of research grants to university workers, not only on an equitable basis, but also so that duplication will be avoided and the most pressing and worthy projects funded. This has been overcome to an extent by the establishment of the Australian Research Grants Committee. However, undoubtedly the most important problem is the likely invasion of state rights by Commonwealth participation in financing; the states want Federal money, but not necessarily spent in the way the Commonwealth decides. Hence, in the university sphere, for example, New South Wales has established its own Universities Board which enables the state to investigate university needs for itself and consult with the Australian Universities Commission on the projects and extent of funding which are necessary. The establishment of advanced education boards in the states has given them similar responsibility in the case of colleges of advanced education. These, therefore, at state level, parallel the Commonwealth's Australian Commission on Advanced Education (ACAE), a board with functions similar to the AUC.

Thus Commonwealth 'intrusion' in the educational field has been, on the one hand, welcomed; on the other, a series of checks and balances has been devised to try and protect state rights. Yet the problem of allocation of sufficient resources for education remains, and there has been much publicity given to the need for more Commonwealth participation (and hence suggestions of greater Commonwealth control) in the educational field. This is all rather natural, despite the constitutional position, because it is the Commonwealth which controls the major financial resources. Further, the tendency in Australian government is very much towards greater centralism, and the concentration of power in Canberra is likely to continue.

Analysis of expenditure   Estimates of total expenditure on education in Australia show that by 1969–70 it stood at $1,287 million.[2] In the public authority sector, expenditure had risen by some 50 per cent since as recently as 1965–6, and in the private sector, while the rise was considerably less, it was significant nevertheless. In 1969–70 Commonwealth expenditure on cash benefits to persons under various sections of the Commonwealth Scholarship Scheme totalled, for postgraduate awards, about $4·5 million, and for undergraduate awards, just over $18 million. This contrasted with the cost of awards for students taking courses in advanced education institutions (a little more than $1·5 million) and tertiary technical scholarships (just over $1 million). At the secondary level the cost of Commonwealth Secondary Scholarship allowances exceeded $6·7 million. For the Commonwealth Soldiers' Children Education Scheme, $3·2

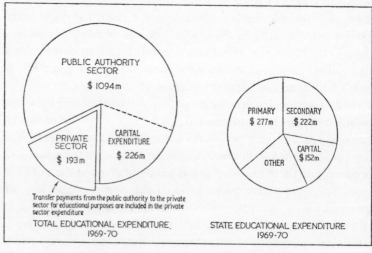

Fig 6   Expenditure on education in Australia

million was provided—it might be noted that Australian repatriation payments for ex-servicemen and their dependents have, as a policy of long standing, always been quite generous.

The Commonwealth role might be put another way. Payments by the Commonwealth to the states specifically for education in the same financial year (1969–70) totalled $148 million, made up of about $77 million for current costs and $71 million for capital expenditure. By far the greater proportion of this amount was earmarked for universities (about $67 million). Next largest beneficiary was the system of colleges of advanced education (about $20 million). To be added, mainly to the university total, was nearly $3·5 million for research. Capital expenditure on technical training amounted to almost $10 million and, in a new departure for Commonwealth assistance, teachers' colleges run by the states obtained capital grants of over $13 million, although no funds were contributed to running expenses of these institutions. Also included in the grand total mentioned was about $900,000 for aboriginal advancement.

The balance was made up of contributions to purely school expenditure. Included under current disbursements was just over $12 million for per capita annual grants for independent schools which, as indicated, were in general sums supplemented by the states. Money made available from capital funds for science laboratories totalled nearly $13 million, a little over half of this sum going to science laboratories for government schools in the states. A sum of $7·5 million was provided for secondary school libraries.

For the 1969–70 financial year the percentage of gross national product spent on education in Australia was estimated at 4·28. This is far from being a high figure, and contemporary criticism (at the time of Australia's active participation in the Vietnam war) that the percentage of GNP spent on defence amounted to 3·47 per cent is pertinent. The situation can be put another way, however; total Commonwealth government expenditure on education approximated $250 million in 1969–70, or nearly 20 per cent of total expenditure on education throughout Australia. It is of interest to note that, of the Commonwealth total, over \$16 million was spent within the Australian Capital Territory, and almost \$7 million on education in the Northern Territory.

The rate of inflation, however, quickly makes financial figures lose some significance. Nevertheless, it should be stated that, of a total expenditure by the states for the same period of about \$925 million, the largest single amount of recurrent expenditure (almost \$278 million) was earmarked for primary schools (including infants' and pre-school education conducted by governments); the next largest sum was, not surprisingly, for secondary education (\$222·7 million). Some lesser amounts of this grand total are of singular interest: administrative and general expenses amounted to only \$21·5 million, less by several millions than, for example, the \$34 million for the transportation of school-children, an annual bill which, as has been seen, is growing steadily. The training of teachers cost, on recurrent funds, not quite \$59 million in 1969–70, while universities needed nearly \$71 million and technical education \$83 million. Only \$4·3 million was earmarked for agricultural and forestry education.

Methods of funding   The constitutional and financial problem which has, of late years, caused most continuous wrangling between Commonwealth and states is the supply of money for recurrent expenditures and development projects. Commonwealth financial hegemony really began with the surrender of taxation powers by the states to the Commonwealth in 1942; the position still is that direct income tax is collected by the Commonwealth, and the states are reimbursed by a formula which is adjusted from time to time. The states are hardly ever satisfied with what they receive, especially in times of acute inflationary trends. Coupled with the increasing community demand for educational services, this situation has reacted to the detriment of state finances, especially when the Commonwealth government announces grants on a dollar-for-dollar basis, which has been its favourite method of offering funds. For the more money the Commonwealth channels into the economy, eventually the more tax it collects, whereas the states (except for indirect taxes which are distinctly limited) continue to be dependent on Commonwealth tax reimbursements and have to meet loan interest charges. The annual pilgrimage of state premiers and treasurers to Canberra for 'the handout' has become, not only monotonous, but often also a degrading spectacle.

Without a more suitable basis for funding, the future for state support of all social services, including education, looks unsatisfactory. On the other hand, year by year the Commonwealth advances more surely into the educational financing field, helping the states here and there, very much on an ad hoc basis. Although it is widely accepted that many of the Commonwealth moves into the educational field were made as a result of election promises (and hence with a view to gaining votes), the fact is that a number of important results and problems have flowed from this shift in attitude. First, there is no doubt at all that Commonwealth intervention was a very good thing for the universities and, subsequent to the adoption of many of the recommendations of the 1964 Martin Report, for an enlarged and more diversified higher education system. Second, he who pays the piper calls the tune, and Commonwealth policy on educational matters must now be regarded seriously. The question of state rights in education is now very fluid and constitutionally the position is obscure. With the 1972 call by the Australian Labor Party for an Australian Education Commission, and similar trends, the possibility of further administrative and financial control from Canberra is open and, indeed, the issue as to whether the centralised systems —and the independent sector—are likely in the long run to succumb to even greater centralisation is a most interesting one. In the third place, the motives for giving Commonwealth aid to education, in the way it has been given, are open to question: Commonwealth Secondary Scholarships are not subject to an economic means test for parents, so that the scheme can be viewed either as a sheer national economic investment, or as financial aid for the middle and upper strata of society which tend to keep their children longer at school than less fortunate parents. Again, providing aid to all independent schools, rather than on a 'needs' basis (for which many would argue), assists wealthy as well as comparatively poor schools, and hence again favours the children of society's middle and upper strata.

Such policies hardly seem in keeping with an egalitarian spirit, or the real needs of a community, which—so the myth has it—Australia has consistently followed since early white settlement. On the other hand, it must be admitted that in one sense at least it is 'fairer' to give to all than to discriminate. It is also cheaper to bolster the independent education sector than to have to meet all educational costs for about 25 per cent of the school population. The basic philosophical argument against the method of aiding education, however, is that all the schemes introduced by the Federal government have been opportunistic, rather than based on a rational and national plan for education.

COMMONWEALTH ROLE IN EDUCATION

Education in Canberra   The Commonwealth-state position in education is reflected in state envy, not only of the extent of Commonwealth resources but also by what it can and does do for education in its own spheres of responsibility. True, Canberra, Australia's capital city, is atypical. It has a population of about 155,000 and by 1980 this is expected to rise to over 300,000. A twentieth-century planned city, Canberra is an architectural and landscaped showpiece, an obvious result of the plan of its architect, Walter Burley Griffin, and more recently of the work of NCDC, the National Capital Development Commission. The beautiful man-made lake which bisects Canberra does not divide the population sociologically, for most of the population is connected with the public service, which is middle class, education conscious and upwardly mobile. It is well-to-do, and proud of its facilities and buildings: the National War Memorial, for example, or the National Library by the lake and the embassies in its hills. Undoubtedly, most inhabitants are well aware of their educational institutions, their fine new government and independent schools, the Australian National University and the Canberra College of Advanced Education—these facilities all contributing in some degree to the high retention rate in the ACT schools. There can be no doubt that there are great advantages for the Australian family which lives in the Australian Capital Territory, although undeniably there are drawbacks. Canberra is said to have a high rate of juvenile delinquency, and there is evidence of a disturbing incidence of mental illness.

From the time the first Commonwealth-built school opened its doors in Canberra, New South Wales has provided the required teaching staff and supervision, and students have followed that state's pattern of education. Now, however, with a school population of nearly 40,000, of whom about 75 per cent are in government institutions, the time has been seen as ripe for the establishment of a Canberra Education Authority, and a Commonwealth Teaching Service has been established. This has been made possible by teacher education courses at the new Canberra College of Advanced Education, and the members of the CTS will serve in Commonwealth territories like the Northern Territory as well as in the Federal capital. The educational divorce from New South Wales has been made possible not only by the growing size of the ACT operation, but also because of parental and other dissatisfaction with New South Wales's education and the existence in Canberra, since 1966, of a Federal Department of Education and Science. Among other functions, this Department has played an important part in the growth of new schools. For instance, the capital city now has the first of its open-plan primary schools and is experimenting with co-operative teaching systems. Senior high schools or colleges, something like the matriculation colleges of Tasmania, are planned. The Commonwealth government first entered the field of school support with offers of interest-free loans to independent schools in Canberra, and these schools have been quick to take advantage of these, and later, benefits.

The Australian National University merits special mention. Financed wholly by the Commonwealth government, it is divided into a School of General Studies (for undergraduate programmes, and formerly called the Canberra University College) and a School of Advanced Studies (for graduate research in fields including biological sciences, chemistry, physical sciences, medicine, Pacific studies and social sciences). The ANU has a worldwide reputation for scholarship and attracts many advanced students and distinguished academic visitors from overseas. Its accommodation and facilities are of very high standard, and places there are eagerly sought.

The Australian Capital Territory has been well provided with pre-school centres, unlike the position in the states. In 1972 there were about 50 pre-school centres, catering for almost 4,000 children, in Canberra and its environs. The Department of Education and Science has also been cognisant of the need to provide facilities in the capital for handicapped children, and for technical and apprenticeship education. In 1965 the Canberra School of Music was established; in 1972 nearly 700 students were enrolled. Various forms of adult or continuing education are also sponsored by the Commonwealth authorities.[3]

Education in other territories   The Department of Education and Science also has responsibility for educational services in the Northern Territory, especially since South Australia announced that it was withdrawing from the scene (an arrangement similar to that between ACT and New South Wales had existed in the Territory). The Territory has many aborigines to provide for, and this is a particular responsibility for the Welfare Branch of the Northern Territory Administration. Generally speaking, a vigorous programme of increasing educational provision both for the white and aboriginal population in the Territory has been put into operation. For example, the Darwin Community College, opened in 1972, is designed to be a comprehensive post-school institution, providing vocational training programmes at sub-professional, apprenticeship and pre-apprenticeship level, and certificate courses in technological and applied sciences. One interesting aspect of the college is designed to be the organisation of refresher and in-service courses; another, the facilities and tutorial assistance for students taking external courses of universities or other institutions. The college cost $4·5 million.

The fact that in connection with the election of December 1972 little criticism was heard of Australian policy in Papua and New Guinea, a trust territory rapidly moving to independence, suggests that Australian efforts to develop social and other services there have been reasonably successful, at least in the eyes of the Australian electorate, if not in those of certain anti-colonialist powers. Education in Papua–New Guinea has developed rapidly, especially in the decade prior to 1972, and Australian Federal government financial contributions have been heavy. The states have also assisted with manpower release, often to the detriment of their own systems of education which have been severely strained during the same period. In particular, primary education has been strengthened, secondary education developed in a quite remarkable fashion, and tertiary education has been expanded from virtually nothing to university, technical institute and teacher education. Much, of course, still has to be done, but Australia has achieved a good deal for this developing area. One of the most heartening indications is the interest being shown by several university departments or faculties of education in undertaking research work on the problems facing Papua–New Guinea, and the enthusiasm of individual members of staff, not only for helping solve the problems often common to developing countries, but also in arousing interest among their own students for the challenges which inevitably face educators in the Asian–Pacific area. Thus, through higher education within Australia, there is hope that, in the near future, more Australians will take a more active interest in the social development of the countries contiguous to their island continent.

Support for ACER   The trend toward educational development over and above that provided by the states is also exemplified by recent activities of the Australian Council for Educational Research (ACER), a portion of whose funds come from
the Commonwealth. Indeed, ACER plays a most important part
in the development of new ideas in Australian education. Its
aims, as an independent organisation, are to promote educational
research and to encourage it in others, to publish the results of
research and make grants towards research projects, and to foster
any worthwhile development in education which it considers
would be of benefit to Australia.[4]

One area in which ACER has been particularly active in recent
years is the teaching of science. Part, at least, of the impetus for
this interest was the development in New South Wales of an
integrated science curriculum for secondary schools following
the reorganisation of secondary education in the early sixties,
with the adoption of the Wyndham Report and comprehensive
secondary education. Triggered by the work of the Nuclear
Research Foundation of the University of Sydney, scientists produced a number of weighty textbooks for the new courses. While
these new courses attempted with some success to provide for
the wide range of individual differences to be found in a comprehensive school, there was soon some doubt expressed about the
degree of integration of individual sciences provided. At about
the same time, other states were reviewing their courses of
secondary study; in South Australia, for instance, a new senior
physics course emerged.

During the period 1966–9 ACER co-operated with the Victorian Universities and Schools Examinations Board in developing the Junior Secondary Science Project (JSSP). The aim of the
project was to develop science learning materials for the first four
years of the secondary school; in other words, 'to develop in
pupils an understanding of the universe as conceived by scientists, some understanding of the nature and the scope of science,
certain skills important to science, and certain attitudes asso-

ciated with science'.[5] Obviously, then, there was an emphasis
extending beyond subject matter to methods of learning and
teaching, and to the development of attitudes. Materials developed were tested in a number of states. The JSSP has now
developed, with Commonwealth government aid, into the Australian Science Education Project (ASEP), and with the co-
operation of all states. This means that ASEP is the first nationally
based curriculum project.

The Australian Science Education Project is also directed to
the first four secondary years. Adopting an environmental
approach, it aims 'to produce suitable evaluative and descriptive
instruments designed for use with project materials; to develop
a model of a teacher education program for the implementation
of project materials in schools, and to establish a resource service
for the developers of project materials and school teachers'.[6]
Emphasis in the project materials is on individual rates of development, optional pursuits, the use of teaching aids like film loops,
films and slides, and on teacher innovation. It is expected the
project will be completed in 1974 but its influence is likely to be
felt long past that date: in the schools, as a means of training
people skilled in curriculum development and evaluation, in
interstate co-operation, and in other curriculum areas. With
ASEP well under way, a National Committee on Social Science
Teaching has been established; its membership includes the
Commonwealth Department of Education and Science, the state
authorities and the Australian Council for Educational Research.
To a long history of concern for psychological and intelligence
testing, ACER now adds curriculum development and appraisal,
and on an Australia-wide perspective, made possible largely
through the help of the national government.

Somehow, the magnificent new buildings of the Canberra College
of Advanced Education, rising rapidly on former grazing land in
Canberra's new suburb of Belconnen, symbolise the growth of
Commonwealth activity in education. College provision for

H

computer studies, new mechanised methods for foreign language teaching and fresh approaches to teacher education reflect, on a single but beautiful site, the spread of Commonwealth concern for educational development in Australia. The generous financial allocations to Canberra CAE suggest to many where the source for further upgrading Australian education is to be found. Can Canberra's educational paradise become the norm for the whole of Australia? Will today's example become tomorrow's expectation?

6
Today and Tomorrow

SINCE the 1930s visitors from overseas have made several criticisms of Australian education. Australians have usually been very quick to show their resentment at short-term visitors telling them 'hometruths' about their country, but this does not of course invalidate the criticisms, especially if the visitors are learned and experienced.

SOME CRITICISMS OF AUSTRALIAN EDUCATION

From overseas   Eminent authority on comparative education Isaac L. Kandel visited Australia for an international education conference in 1937, and took the opportunity to survey Australian education. In his subsequent book *Types of Administration* Kandel's main criticism concerned the deleterious effect of centralised educational administration which leads to inevitable 'rule by a bureaucracy', sacrificing progress in education 'at the altar of efficiency' and resulting in a 'feeling of complacency'.[1] Centralisation, Kandel observed, meant that inspection and seniority ruled the educational scene, and resulted in the triumph of mediocrity.[2] Significantly, his chapter on Australia and New Zealand was headed 'Education for Efficiency'.

In 1952 H. C. Dent, then editor of *The Times Educational Supplement*, visited Australia. His criticisms included the 'baneful' effects of 'the examination system upon teaching methods in all subjects, but especially practical and craft subjects', and inspection procedures for the promotion and appointment of teachers which precluded 'exploration and experiment'.[3] Dent saw three major reforms as being necessary: 'Promotion of teachers by merit must supplant promotion by seniority'; 'Teachers must become convinced that they are not only free to experiment, but be actively encouraged to do so', and 'the stranglehold of examinations on the schools must be broken'.[4]

Undoubtedly the best known overseas criticism of Australian education was that by Professor R. Freeman Butts, from Teachers' College, Columbia University, who visited Australia in 1954. Much of what he said then is, unfortunately, still valid. In his *Assumptions Underlying Australian Education* Butts was careful to put his remarks within a definite frame of reference; indeed, his criticisms were offered almost apologetically. He was severe about the administration and control of Australian education, about the educational programme itself and especially about teaching methods. He was devastating about the teaching profession. He echoed Dent's criticism that the Australian education systems seemed to 'miss something of the vitality, initiative, creativeness and variety that would come if the doors and windows of discussion and decision were kept more open all the way up and down the educational edifice'.[5] He sought 'a general awakening of local community life' leading to the school becoming 'a genuinely creative agency'.[6] He had grave doubts about the dual system of government and non-government schools: 'insofar as a dual system of schools helps to create and perpetuate class, religious or economic divisions in society . . . and maintain feelings of superiority and inferiority, and insofar as the competition among schools is primarily directed toward the passing of external examinations' he thought it dangerous.[7] Religion, Butts felt, was likely to plague Australian education for years to come. He was critical, as Dent and Kandel had been, of the examination system and of teachers' concern for standards. He was also critical of the effect of inbreeding and other aspects of teacher education.[8]

The assessment of a Canadian, R. W. B. Jackson, was made in

1960. He supported much of what Butts had said a few years before. In addition, he stressed the greater financial commitment to education which he felt would have to be made in Australia. 'Unless the financial and other resources for education are provided on a proper scale', Jackson said, 'a generation of Australian children will have been sold short and denied their educational birthright.'[9] Despite the Australian emphasis on educational equality, Jackson's impression was that this ideal fell far short of what it ought to be at the upper levels of education, including the higher reaches of the secondary school. Insufficient use, he felt, was being made of the talent available. As he saw them, the 'major emergent needs' of Australian education were: greater public interest in, and support for, education; more finance for education; the establishment of clear priorities in education; the decentralisation of educational administration, and more educational research.[10]

Criticism from within Australia   It is easy enough for the outsider to criticise Australian education, but relatively difficult for informed Australians to do so. The foundation of the Australian College of Education in 1959 opened up a possible avenue of professional criticism of the more responsible kind. It is significant that each conference of this body receives a good press and that, following each annual meeting, assessments and criticisms of Australian education have been published in book form, along with research reports and historical-comparative studies. But incisive criticism and suggestion from the ACE have been muted; it has become more of an 'establishment' body in education.

Other than the Knibbs-Turner Report on New South Wales education in the first years of the century, probably one of the earliest well-publicised criticisms of Australian education from within the country came from the first director of the Australian Council for Educational Research, Dr K. S. Cunningham, in 1936. He made a plea for more autonomy, greater flexibility, more exploration and experiment, and the building up of a strong public opinion on the subject of education within Australia. He thought that there was a need for the continuous study of educational problems as a whole, for better material conditions and aids for teaching, for higher professional status and standards, for less formalism in school work, and for attention to be paid to the cultivation of intelligent citizenship.[11]

In 1956 Cramer and Browne (the latter an Australian) in their *Contemporary Education* expressed a need for a clear statement of educational objectives in Australian education:

> Australia has need for the formulation or evolution of an educational philosophy of its own which will embody the characteristics of its own mode of life, its cultural ideas, and national aims. This is particularly the case since Australia has begun to realize that, although her cultural heritage came from western Europe, geographically she is part of Southeast Asia.[12]

Shortly afterwards, the professor of education at the University of Sydney, W. F. Connell, emphasised the social tasks of secondary education and the rapid need for cultural adjustment.[13] He clearly saw the changing nature of secondary education, with the growth in numbers of students staying longer at school. He spoke of the 'heritage of behaviour' being as important as the 'heritage of knowledge'; 'the purposes of secondary education', Connell wrote, 'are more properly defined by a statement about the kind of person, rather than the kind of knowledge, that ought to be built up during adolescence'.[14] What Connell was arguing was the need for a theoretical framework for educational development, first delineating the role of tradition in secondary education, then involving democracy and its implications for the secondary school and, third, incorporating the nature of adolescence and its developmental tasks. According to Connell, three functional tasks which should govern the secondary school are the fulfilment of its roles as a transitional community, as an integrating community, and as a working community.[15]

Economists, too, have had their say about aspects of Australian education. Professor P. H. Karmel, significantly now chairman

of the Australian Universities Commission and also chairman
of the Interim Australian Schools Commission, in the early
sixties pointed to the very low proportion of GNP spent on
education in Australia. He also compared the taxation rates of
various countries as a proportion of their GNP; the inference
was that there was considerable economic room for greater
spending on educational services in Australia.[16]

There have, of course, been many other criticisms by Australians of various aspects of education. For example, Professor
G. W. Bassett of the University of Queensland has pointed to
defects in the preparation of teachers, while Professor W. G.
Walker of the University of New England, authority on educational administration, has been particularly severe on the
deleterious effects of centralisation.[17] Phillip Hughes, of Canberra College of Advanced Education, also writing on the administration of education in Australia, has said:

> The views held on the state education systems owe more to slogans
> and stereotypes than to objective analysis and investigation. On
> the one hand they are pilloried as vast juggernauts without human
> concern, necessarily evil because of their centralization of author-
> ity and their size. On the other, they are upheld as the necessary
> instruments for obtaining both efficiency of administration and,
> more importantly, equality, and quality of educational oppor-
> tunity on a state-wide basis.[18]

In his preface to the same book, *School, College and University:
The Administration of Education in Australia*, Walker expanded
thus:

> The administration and organisation of education in Australia
> have long attracted the attention of critics both from overseas and
> from within Australia itself. No sector has escaped the lash. The
> government schools are accused of breeding mediocrity and
> conformity, of emphasizing efficiency rather than 'education', of
> authoritarianism and bureaucratic control. The non-government
> schools, on the other hand, are accused of shirking responsibility
> for that leadership which their freedom should grant them in

producing change. Indeed, they are accused of remaining islands
of conservatism in a sea of change.

Nor has higher education escaped. Teachers' colleges are
described as inward looking, inbred, merely leading their students
to become departmental stereotypes. The technical and agricultural colleges are often seen as low level training institutions
dominated by the government departments which are responsible
for them.[19]

Harsh words, but sufficient smoke to suggest at least a smoulder-
ing fire of criticism.

THE PRESENT SITUATION

Questioning educational policies   Certainly, all is not well
with Australian education. Despite progress and change, many
are dissatisfied with what they see or experience. There is more
satisfaction with infants' grades—and somewhat less with primary
schools for, even here, criticism is heard—than with secondary,
technical or tertiary education. And it is in the secondary schools
and universities where student dissatisfaction has become vocal,
usually reasonably muted but occasionally violent. Research evidence from the Australian National University and from Sydney
University suggests that up to a quarter of secondary school
students are bored or hate school, and up to another 50 per cent
are indifferent to their school life.[20] Student activism at secondary
level has been marked in Victoria and, at the time of writing, is
nascent in New South Wales. There is no doubt that, increasingly,
students are questioning 'the system'. And it is the system, too,
to which state teachers object, since in their ranks as well there
is much dissatisfaction with bureaucratic control, curricula and
the effect of examinations. The usual cry is that much more
money should be spent on Australian education, as if money were
the panacea for all ills. The position is clearly compounded by
Commonwealth and state government spending on grants to
independent schools; so prevalent has this become and so worried
about it are state school teachers and parents who support the
government systems, that an organisation known as DOGS

(Organisation for the Defence of Government Schools) has been formed and has become politically active on this single issue, to the extent of polling rather well in some state elections. Dissatisfaction with educational policies is widespread. Education, as well as being a heavy budget claimant at state level, and increasingly at Commonwealth level also, is now regarded by many as a leading political issue.

Progress in South Australia   Is the present situation, however, really as bad as some of the critics maintain? Consider South Australia. In the nineteenth century, South Australia gained a reputation for being the 'granary of Australia'; in more recent years the state's pastoral and agricultural pursuits have diversified and the rate of industrialisation has been very marked. South Australia's progress in education has also been notable. It has been marked by vigour and drive, considerable innovation and a pleasing increase in the degree of community involvement. Some notable features of that state's education include a high secondary school retention rate, by Australian standards relatively good provision for pre-school education, experiments with open classrooms and ungrading (especially at primary grade levels), direct representation for secondary students on high school councils, the appointment of teacher aides and an improved teacher supply position.[21] This last characteristic warrants the observation that South Australia has pursued vigorously a policy of additional teachers' college provision of a high order, co-operation with the new Flinders University of South Australia in teacher education, and the recruitment of skilled personnel for teacher education from other states and countries.

These are notable achievements, but perhaps the most important change has been the emergence of a more enlightened administrative élite in education, especially with the recent response to the Karmel Report and the invitation by the director-general of education for more freedom, independence and professional responsibility to be shown by teachers. Yet for a state with more than a million people, and with nearly 300,000 students at school, problems remain. Despite the innovations mentioned there are still secondary school problems of 'tracking' (a form of streaming), and the qualifications of some teachers are still only marginally professional, a backlog from earlier days when South Australia merely followed practices in other states.

The situation in New South Wales   By way of contrast, the experience of New South Wales, with nearly one million students in school, may be cited. In the fifteen years or so after World War II, the state gained a reputation for progressive educational development: the division of the state school system into administrative areas, progressive curriculum revision, a lengthy survey of the need for secondary school reorganisation, and the implementation of recommendations, the development of extensive guidance and research services, and so on.

During the 1960s, however, the system grew even more heavily in numbers of students, but not sufficiently in teachers, and in conflict between the powerful NSW Teachers' Federation and the state Department of Education. Currently, therefore, the state has an educational system, on the one hand generally agreed to be too large and administered too bureaucratically by cumbersome government machinery involving a number of government departments and, on the other, criticised continually by a teachers' union which makes little attempt to extend the professional education and attitudes of its members, and which apparently delights in providing a continual flow of criticism of everything the state government does—or more usually does not do—in the field of educational policy. Although sheer size exacerbates problems (the numbers sitting for external examinations, for example) there are signs of continuing growth and experiment. Curriculum revision continues, and in new courses centrally designed there is a trend to less prescription as to what is to be taught; experiments in primary school social science teaching are actively encouraged, and there is increasing evidence of state secondary schools actually being exhorted to develop unique patterns of intra-school organisation. With the reintroduction of government financial aid for independent schools, a small number of experimental, progressive schools (mainly for primary children) have appeared. However, purely political 'gimmicks' like the extension of free transport for schoolchildren tend to preoccupy political minds, rather than basic educational questions.

Secondary experiment in Tasmania Altogether, Tasmania has fewer than 100,000 students in school, with a smaller proportion in non-government schools than on the mainland. Tasmania is also less industrialised than the other states; hence finance for social services is more of a problem. Nevertheless, as has been stressed, the state has a reputation for educational experiment, especially at secondary level. In the 1930s the area school movement received wide publicity, its aim being the provision of relevant educational content, through activity methods, for the bulk of rural students of secondary age. Subsequently, Tasmania pressed ahead with a network of high schools, and recently has established some matriculation colleges to provide a different ethos and atmosphere, more suitable discipline and improved staff-student relationships for the last two years of secondary schooling. No doubt this is significant, both as a guide to the other states, and also because Tasmania has the lowest student retention rate of any state educational system in Australia.

Western Australian difficulties Reference has been made to Australia's smallest state, but what of the largest, Western Australia? In the east, where most of Australia's population resides, little is known of the west, except that it is vast in size, many settlements are extremely isolated, rich mineral deposits are being opened up, and railways and settlements built. Educationally, probably the only fact most easterners know is that the University of Western Australia (in Perth) is the first and only completely free Australian university. What they do not know is that Western Australia has worked hard to spread the opportunity for secondary education as widely as resources will allow and that reorganisation of this stage of the educational ladder has involved the opening of comprehensive high schools, with curricular levels very much like the NSW Wyndham Plan, and a basic core curriculum for adolescents. This has been achieved by a paternal type of central administration which, among other things, has provided textbooks and materials for students on a very wide and non-commercial basis. When one looks further afield than schools, one observes not only the Western Australia Institute of Technology (WAIT) which is growing rapidly in numbers, but also the embryonic Murdoch University, also in the Perth area, to provide the state's second university.

Whatever the criticisms of educational administration and organisation in Western Australia, however, there can be no gainsaying the fact that the problem of distance and difficulties in spreading educational opportunity have been very great indeed: the state has an area of 975,000 square miles, the population is only 1 million strong, there are about 800 schools (600 of which are government controlled) and little more than 220,000 students of whom government schools cater for 180,000.

Need for balanced assessment   Any assessment of the present situation in Australian education must therefore balance what has been achieved in the face of difficulties against the shortcomings observed. By virtue of their claim for more Federal funds for education, state authorities admit that deficiencies exist, but at the same time rightly claim credit for many achievements and many examples of progress. After all, for a long time they have waged the main battle for more schools, teachers and equipment, at the same time seeking to implement policies attuned to extending equality and opportunity.

INFLUENCING EDUCATIONAL POLICY— GROUPS WITH AN INTEREST

The state bureaucracies   Although it seems that teacher organisations can and do spend large sums criticising government policy and actions in education—especially prior to elections, both state and federal—education departments make serious efforts to publicise government achievements, new policies and progress, but always on a distinctly limited budget. For example, some states have produced films for commercial distribution, while others have concentrated on press releases, information sheets and booklets for public circulation. Rather naturally, these publicity materials give prominence to achievements and, to the extent that difficulties and problem areas are not spoken about, slant the items towards a favourable, but apparently objective, impression of what a particular government is doing. It has been rare for any educational self-examination in public to take place; ministers have seemed to be intent, even in answering parliamentary questions, on avoiding difficult issues. There are signs, nevertheless, of more openness, with the proliferation of reports on education in the states: the Tasmanian *School in Society* Report of 1968, the Western Australian Dettman Report of 1969, the 1970 Radford Report on Queensland education, and the Karmel Report in South Australia. With the growth in administrative bureaucracy, much of the time of senior administrative officers appears to be taken with keeping a minister out of trouble, even to the extent of keeping him at times out of the limelight. (On the other hand, a pleasing feature of educational offices today is the frequency with which increasing numbers of administrators are able to travel overseas.) Thus, Australian parents are often not as well served by their politicians or professional educators as they might be, and their attention is attracted by criticisms levelled by trade-union-minded teacher organisations. An unfortunate sidelight to this situation is the existence of public service regulations which, in most states, prevent government employees, as individuals, from speaking out on educational questions. It keeps trouble from the door of officialdom, but puts most educational criticism out of public earshot or, at least, into low key.

Public service regulations relating to statements criticising government education policy by teachers or departmental administrators are, in general, very strict in Australia. Even directors-general are not frequently quoted in the press and official statements are usually attributed to 'a spokesman'. Similarly, ministers for education usually restrict themselves to obviously prepared statements, even in parliament, and are assisted in their utterances by a staff of 'ghost writers' or private secretaries. Thus, although the majority of statements on education (or, more correctly, on educational shortcomings) seem to emanate from teachers' organisations and professors of education, on occasion the director-general may speak out in a calculated way on a particular issue or the minister may make an off-the-cuff statement. Although examples of this are forthcoming, it should be noted that these statements are comparatively rare, since education is a contentious issue; the large bureaucracies do not look for trouble and are likely to prefer 'no comment'.

Two examples of ministerial off-the-cuff and calculated statements are, however, worth mentioning. The first, which occurred quite some time ago, concerned a minister for education of a certain state who made a world trip during the parliamentary recess. His stated purpose was to investigate educational developments in a large number of overseas systems. On his return, he contented himself with a single pronouncement: 'Our system of education, I am convinced, is the best in the world'. Not surprisingly, in a country where outspoken utterances on educational questions constitute a comparatively new phenomenon and inbreeding is common, there was little comment on this assessment, and even less on the value for taxpayers' money! A second example is rather more recent. A new Victorian minister for education published a book, *Looking Ahead in Education*, in which he actually openly criticised and commented upon the school scene and made suggestions for future changes.[22]

Government is often hesitant to speak its mind on educational issues; nevertheless, there is some evidence that this situation is changing. In the general climate of centralised education systems, the teacher organisations perform a useful, if at times unpalatable, task of prompting; the trouble is that government departments, always short of money and time, are unwilling, and frequently unable, to spend a great deal of either in replying to criticism, and in some quarters think that it is unnecessary to do so. What professional educators often consider a pity is that the teacher organisations do not themselves spend more money, time and attention on the further education of their own members—'professional' journals are generally of poor quality, and the attitudes expressed in them partisan rather than objective. Governments, too, should be more energetic in selling pride in Australian educational achievements, some of which are notable, innovative and extremely interesting. What worries some observers is that criticism of Australian education (often well deserved and given most vocally by teachers' organisations) is tending to get out of hand.

The work of teacher organisations   The role of teacher organisations in the history of education in Australia has been an important one. Government teachers in each state long ago formed a union or association: in New South Wales the Teachers' Federation consists of a strong amalgam of a large number of associations based either on geographical location or allied interest (there is, for instance, a principals' association). Years ago, the several state bodies formed the Australian Teachers' Federation, but real power remains with the state organisations: the NSW Federation, for example, has had a high degree of influence, whereas its monolithic force is not reflected in Victoria where the teachers' union has split into a number of different groups. Over the years, these organisations have been concerned mainly with effecting improvements in teachers' salary scales. To a great extent they have been successful in this. Other prime interests have been the working conditions of teachers, including criticism of class sizes, the standard of school buildings, promotions opportunities and the difficulties of technical and teacher education. Generally well-organised, with an increasing predisposition to militancy among their leaders, these organisations have resorted to direct action, frequent and well-publicised criticism of education departments and governments, and have maintained close links with the trade union movement. Paying professional organisers and unashamedly attempting to influence voting patterns, the unions have attracted considerable publicity. Their principal target has always been non-Labor governments: in New South Wales, for example, relations between the Teachers' Federation and Liberal-Country Party Coalition have been extremely strained, even hostile, in marked contrast to their contacts with the previous Labor government.

The role of parents   The rise in parental concern for education has been reflected in the media, rather than by concerted public action by parent organisations which, in general, are lightly supported and, regrettably, often find their activities confined to raising money for schools. It could be surmised that this parental negligence stems from the old Australian disposition to look to the government for all help, and is also reflected in the poor development of forms of local government in Australia. This is not to say that some parents and citizens groups, parent and friend associations, or school councils are not extremely active, but they are the exception rather than the rule. In both the case of parent groups associated with government schools and those connected with independent ones, national bodies exist, and they see their lobbying role as important, but to date they receive little publicity. They are certainly neither as militant nor as effective as teacher organisations. State government attitudes to these organisations vary, in some states useful co-operation being possible. The view that parents in general are apathetic is accepted by most educational administrators. The notable exception to this is the strength shown by Catholic parents.

Some take exception to the fund-raising role of parent bodies on grounds other than that they should be more concerned with policy. There has been a tendency by educational authorities to subsidise from consolidated revenue funds money raised by parent groups; the argument against this is that parent bodies in wealthy suburbs, or representative of wealthy schools, can raise more money and hence attract greater government subsidies, hence their socio-economic ascendancy vis-à-vis schools in poorer circumstances is enhanced. The subsidy system encourages *in*-equality. The overriding importance of fund-raising is aptly reflected in the fact that the only mention parent associations receive in any of the state yearbooks is in this role.

The position of the Roman Catholic Church   The crisis which Roman Catholic schools have had to meet has been severe. Fewer Catholic children are attending church schools (about 60 per cent now compared with 70 per cent or more a few years ago), conditions in the schools are admitted to be unfavourable in comparison with, for example, class sizes and equipment in government schools, and the shortage of religious for teaching duties has been met, with difficulty, by the recuitment of lay teachers. Despite mounting aid from governments, various options have been considered by Catholic authorities. One direc-tor of Catholic education suggested that the church should eventually withdraw from the educational scene, but he was promptly returned to parish duties by his archbishop. Neverthe-less, several schemes for modification of the traditional Catholic role have been aired, including restricting enrolments to those children whose parents really value a religious education for their young, and withdrawing from certain rungs (for example, the senior secondary years) of the educational ladder. So far, the most significant modification seems to have been the closure of small rural secondary schools; but perhaps in the long run equally important is the slowing (in places, halting) of church school building. A fair estimate seems to be that the 'system' of Catholic education might well have completely crumbled had it not been for the extensive government aid which in the Common-wealth's case in 1972 envisaged paying—in conjunction with the states—up to 40 per cent of the running costs of all independent schools. A large part of the cost of school financing is the in-

I

creasing bill for salaries. This will rise further if the trend towards not only lay teachers, but also lay principals, continues.
Fees vary with the religious order running a school, and with the
locality and the type of socio-economic group patronising it, but
in general fees are very much lower than in the case of other
independent schools. They range from possibly less than $20
per term for a primary child to over $70 for a senior secondary
student. It must, however, be remembered that these are basic
fees and that parents may claim tax relief on any such fees up to
a certain maximum.

Concern of the Commonwealth government   The
avowed objective of the Commonwealth government's Secondary Scholarship Scheme is to encourage the retention at school
for the last two secondary years of students with very high
academic promise. At the time, the opponents of the move suggested that it was politically motivated; more recently, criticism
has been levelled at the discrimination the scheme causes.
According to one of the best known contemporary commentators
of Australian education, H. P. Schoenheimer: 'Statistically, the
students of the inner-suburban school are going to gain five
scholarships, with a total value over two years of $2,500; and the
students of the very wealthy [that is, independent] school will
be awarded 24 scholarships with a total value of $19,200'.[23] He
claims that pupils attending state schools win 1 Commonwealth
Secondary scholarship for every 16 eligible students, whereas
students attending Catholic schools win 1 for every 12, and non-
Catholic non-state schools 1 for every 7. Other available evidence suggests that schools in lower socio-economic areas and
in rural districts fare very much worse than even the inner city
state school. The emoluments provided for scholarship winners
are handsome, but clearly the arrangement favours the socio-
economically advantaged student. Scholarships are awarded on
the results of a special test battery developed for the purpose;
the tests cover scientific and quantitative thinking, the humanities and written expression, and no specific preparation is neces-

sary for them. As Schoenheimer suggests, a useful by-product of this unjust scholarship arrangement is the construction of tests which could be used across state borders for other purposes.

With the knowledge that the extent of public debt in the states is growing so large while that of the Commonwealth is growing ever smaller, the Commonwealth is clearly concerned about financial relationships with the states; its decision to establish a centre at the Australian National University in Canberra for the study of these relationships is an indication. Yet this is but one aspect of a growing Commonwealth concern for equality and opportunity in Australian education. The CSS scheme may foster inequalities (and, hence, more opportunity for an élite), but several other Commonwealth activities which do add a measure of equality to the various educational systems in Australia have been mentioned in previous pages. In the future, these latter activities would seem likely to be extended, as the concluding section of this chapter indicates.

LOOKING TO THE FUTURE

A changing scene   The changes in, and major problems of, Australian education are typified by the movement towards a mass system of post-secondary education. Speaking at the University of Melbourne in June 1972, Sir Hugh Ennor, Secretary of the Federal Department of Education and Science, pointed to the great enrolment increases in the final year of secondary school and highlighted this very problem.[24] He pointed out that in Victoria alone only 600 students were enrolled in the final secondary school grade in government schools in 1947, whereas in 1971 this number had increased to 11,500 in government schools alone, and that the comparable figures for the whole of Australia showed a rise from 6,100 to 45,000 in a twenty-year period. In his calculation, only 15,000 of the 45,000 could be accounted for by sheer population increase. He also estimated that over the next ten years there would be an increase of about 50 per cent in the enrolments of both schools and post-secondary

educational institutions. W. D. Borrie's demographic projections
substantiate this forecast. He indicates that 45 per cent of males
aged seventeen and over were participating in secondary education in 1971, and that this was likely to rise to 52 per cent by
1981.[25] The corresponding figures for females are 32 and 43 per
cent. Put another way, whereas in 1969 there were 369,000
secondary students aged fifteen or more, by 1976 the total in
this category will be 507,000, and in 1986 it will have reached
629,000. Thus, estimates of tertiary education students in Australia (assuming constant enrolment rates after 1970) show that
whereas 213,000 were projected for 1971 (the actual figure was
211,500) by 1976 the total is likely to grow to 260,000, and to
304,000 by 1981 and 324,000 by 1986. Over this period the rise
in tertiary students *other than* university enrolments should be
from 98,000 in 1971 to 148,000 in 1981 and 164,000 in 1986.

It is in this situation, Ennor emphasised, that mass post-
secondary education has come to stay, 'a system in which there
is a variety of institutions offering courses at a variety of levels'.[26]
Thus, although Ennor estimated that probably not more than
15 per cent of the 18–21 age group in Australia were receiving
higher education, compared with almost 50 per cent in the USA,
present trends suggest that Australia is moving steadily towards
the American situation. The problem therefore becomes one of
what 'proportion of available and national resources . . . should
be devoted to providing opportunities and facilities for tertiary
education',[27] especially since Australia seems to be in a state of
moving away from a restrictive or élitist higher education
system. Already, as we have seen, diversification is taking place,
and it is costing great sums of money. Where is additional finance
to come from? Is there a limit? Which are the most urgent
priorities?

Ennor's address was deliberately and refreshingly provocative.
He attacked the long-established priority of reducing class sizes
in schools and showed that, for every reduction of one student
per class, the annual cost (omitting capital expenditure) would

be $25 million extra on the education bill. He showed that this money could be utilised better in other ways. He also asserted, what is sometimes forgotten, that the secondary school's role is changing, since more enrolments mean a broader spectrum of student expectations and abilities. With the growth of a mass post-secondary system, too, there will be a need for more flexibility among institutions of higher and further education, and this, Ennor believed, was a problem that as yet was far from solved. As well as involving altered university attitudes towards flexibility, there was a need for a change in social attitudes generally towards colleges and universities.

Among Ennor's provocative comments were suggestions that university courses might profitably be shortened, that a multi-level polytechnic system (somewhat on British lines) might solve some problems, and that nobody should forget that additional financial resources would not only be demanded by tertiary education, but by all sections of education from the pre-school upwards. He also considered that there was probably some limit on the amount of educational expansion the country could stand and hence a likely need for more efficiency in the spending of the educational dollar.

The changing scene also incorporates alterations in the composition and attitudes of the teaching profession. As R. T. Fitzgerald indicates, teachers as a group have become younger—nearly half of them are under thirty-five.[28] Inevitably, this must change the attitudes of teachers as a whole, both professionally and industrially. The profession has also come to rely heavily on female recruitment, and this suggests a higher rate of turnover of staff, and heavier problems of retraining when women teachers return from a period of homemaking. Teaching may well become one of the first nationally important occupations to be dominated by women. Fitzgerald also emphasises the militant attitude already being shown by some teachers' unions to inspection policies, and to an extent changes in these reflect altered attitudes by teachers at the professional level. In the future, the profession's outlook may well be considerably different from what the public has experienced in the past.

Federal politics and education, 1972   Probably for the first time, the Australian Federal election campaign of late 1972 saw education as a major, if not the most important, issue, apart from the question of national leadership.[29] The government of the day (Liberal–Country parties) believed that it had done much: 'as financier and innovator, the Commonwealth is providing the impetus in Australian education'. In election publicity, the governing parties stressed their belief in extending educational opportunity and improving standards, and pointed to educational achievements like aboriginal education, migrants, scholarships, assistance for teacher education, and educational research and curriculum development. They opposed the centralisation of education in Canberra, supporting on the other hand a policy of diversity, variety and autonomy for as many educational institutions as possible.

The principal opposition party, the Australian Labor Party, took the lead in the early part of the election campaign in highlighting education as a major issue. Its main promises were to spend much more money on education, establish a Schools Commission to assess national education needs and recommend action on them, establish a pre-schools commission in order to provide Commonwealth-wide pre-school facilities, abolish fees at institutions of tertiary education, establish 'open' tertiary institutions to provide for people who have missed educational opportunities, and arrange special help for minority and disadvantaged groups. The Labor Party was pledged to the continuance of government aid for independent schools, as were the government parties, but less was heard of Labor's internal dispute over whether this aid should be on a 'needs' basis. It was clear that both government and opposition were aware of the importance of the Roman Catholic vote on the question of 'state aid'. In New South Wales, by way of contrast, the Council for the Defence of Government Schools, being 'positively orientated to our community schools, the children who attend them and the teachers who serve in them', mounted candidates in key electorates and strenuously opposed 'state aid'. DOGS had already had a measure of publicity and success in state elections, and obviously represented clear, if naive, opposition to wealthy independent schools which, it believed, were becoming more favoured through Federal aid to *all* independent schools.

The question of high fee schools attracted opposition from other smaller parties, none of whom had representatives in the Federal lower house. Of these groups, the most influence was exerted by the Australia Party (a new organisation, thought to be largely composed of intellectuals and disenchanted government supporters) and the Democratic Labor Party (the result of the 1955 Labor split, and thought to be heavily representative of Catholic political interests). The Australia Party declared itself in favour of a national education system, spending more of the national wealth on education, a Commonwealth Education Commission with the power of financial allocation, decentralisation of administration through regional authorities, a greater role for parents, and equality of opportunity for, rather than equal treatment of, students. This party was against the dual system of schools, and proposed a policy of conditional aid whereby 'only schools which are prepared to accept and cater for children of any religious or social background will be eligible for aid'. The Democratic Labor Party wanted improved scholarship conditions at tertiary institutions and priority for the development of colleges of advanced education; for primary and secondary education the party favoured continuance of state aid but on a more generous formula, and generally laid great stress on the parents' right of freedom of choice for the education of their children.

A new era?   On 2 December 1972 the Australian electorate went to the polls. The Liberal–County Party coalition government of rather conservative complexion, which had governed Australia since 1949, was defeated and the Australian Labor Party, led by Mr Gough Whitlam, took office. The new Prime

Minister wasted no time in implementing his party's policies: as
well as recognition of the People's Republic of China and the
abolition of conscription, an interim schools commission and a
pre-schools commission which had been promised in his policy
speech were established. In a nationwide telecast shortly after
assuming office, Mr Whitlam said that he believed the 'futile
debate' on state aid and state rights in education was ended with
the appointment of the schools commission and that a new era
was dawning for Australian social life generally. Before the
month was out, the new minister for education was planning a
thousand-strong teacher task force funded by Federal finance
which would aid schools in Papua–New Guinea and poorly
staffed Australian schools, the introduction of a supplementary
spending scheme to help the states in immediate major difficulties, continuing support for fee-paying private schools, and
strong measures to curb graduate unemployment.[30] A brisk
start, without doubt, for a future full of challenge and interest.

Many Australians hope that the new government will be more
successful than past administrations in furthering the cause of
aboriginal rights, including those of a decent education. In the
face of comparative neglect, the threat of black militancy is increasing. Although in towns and cities aboriginal children attend
schools with other Australian children, and special schools exist
in isolated areas and on mission stations, the facts are that the
attendance of aboriginal children is often irregular, home and
nutrition conditions bad, and most aboriginal students leave
school by fifteen. Very few proceed to tertiary education. Various
forms of financial assistance are available, but the problem of
securing satisfactory social and living conditions for these people
has yet to be solved. State governments provide special schemes
of financial assistance for aborigines; in 1968 the Commonwealth
instituted a special study grants scheme for aboriginal post-
secondary education, and in 1970 a secondary scholarship
scheme to encourage retention at school after the minimum
leaving age. Yet much remains to be done, for assistance for

aborigines does not compare favourably with, for example, the aid given under the Colombo and other plans to overseas students who study at institutions of tertiary education in Australia.

IN CONCLUSION

This brief review has endeavoured to show how Australian schools, colleges and universities have developed, how authorities have met the challenges of a changing and expanding post-war Australia, and something of the achievements, problems and criticisms of yesterday and today, with a hint of what the morrow might bring. Throughout, emphasis has been placed on the twin goals of equality and opportunity, goals which it seems in the Australian context are indisputably linked. The approach has been essentially political, and for good reason. It has often been said that Australians are over governed, but it certainly seems to be the expectation that educational progress in the future will be as much the result of government action, as of the community's sense of justice and fair play. Certain it is that the Australian student of today has a ladder to climb, infinitely better placed and more convenient than that of his predecessor a century ago, but it seems a reasonable forecast that Australians will continue— through their governments—to pursue still greater equality of opportunity and seek fulfilment of their aspirations, whatever, in the uncertain future, these may turn out to be.

Notes

Chapter 1

1 Austin, A. G. *Australian Education 1788–1900* (Melbourne, 1961), 14
2 Austin, 35
3 Crawford, R. M. *Australia* (1960, 5th imp), 86
4 Ward, Russel. *The Australian Legend* (Melbourne, 1966), 71
5 Ward, 117
6 Barcan, Alan. *A Short History of Education in New South Wales* (Sydney, 1965), 150
7 For a full review see Austin (above), Chapters 6 and 7. For documentary evidence relating to this period see also Austin, A. G. *Select Documents in Australian Education 1788–1900* (Melbourne, 1963) and Griffiths, D. C. *Documents on the Establishment of Education in New South Wales 1789–1800* (Melbourne, 1957)
8 A succinct review of secondary education in the nineteenth centurn is provided by *Report of the Committee Appointed to Survey Secondary Education in New South Wales*, H. S. Wyndham, Chairman (Sydney, 1958), Chapter 1 (known as the Wyndham Report)
9 For details of the reforms touching secondary education in New South Wales during this period see Crane, A. R. & Walker, W. G. *Peter Board: His Contribution to the Development of Education in New South Wales* (Melbourne, 1957), and Wyndham Report *loc cit*

Chapter 2

1 The basic statistics which follow are most easily obtained by reference to *Official Year Book of the Commonwealth of Australia*, Bureau of Census and Statistics (various years); or to *Education News*, Department of Education and Science
2 Lynch, P. 'Women's Role in Immigration', Ministerial Statement (Canberra, 1970), 7

3 For details, see *Commonwealth Year Book* (1971). See also Lynch, P. *Immigration in the 1970s* (Canberra, 1970)

4 Commonwealth Statistician. *Quarterly Summary of Australian Statistics*, no 283 (Canberra, March 1972)

5 Augimeri, P. M. 'Immigration: Areas of Debate', quoting Hall, A. R., 216–17 in Arndt, H. W. & Boxer, A. H. (eds) *The Australian Economy* (Melbourne, 1972), 205–23

6 Cowan, R. W. T. (ed) *Education for Australians* (Melbourne, 1964), Introduction

7 McDonnell, R. M., Radford, W. C. & Staurenghi, P. M. *Review of Education in Australia 1948–54* (Melbourne, 1956), xii, xiii

8 Cole, P. R. *The Rural School in Australia* (Melbourne, 1937), 11

9 Browne, G. S. 'State Education over Fifty Years', *Education News*, 3, no 2 (April 1951), 8

10 Wheelwright, E. L. (ed). *Higher Education in Australia* (Melbourne, 1965), 64

11 McDonnell, *et al*, 179

12 Education Department, Tasmania. *The Tasmanian Area School* (Hobart, 1942)

13 Cole, 10

14 See Chapter 1, n 8. Chapter 4 of the Wyndham Report details the changes recommended

15 For further details, see McDonnell, *et al*, 38–41

16 Committee on Australian Universities. *Report of the Committee on Australian Universities*. K. A. H. Murray, Chairman (Canberra, 1957)

17 Commonwealth of Australia. *Tertiary Education in Australia*. Report of the Committee on the Future of Tertiary Education in Australia to the Australian Universities Commission. L. H. Martin, Chairman. 3 vols (Canberra, 1964 & 1965)

18 See *Education News*, February issues. Of the total of 36,370 (23,342 women) for 1970, NSW had 11,547 students, Victoria 12,916, Queensland 3,925, South Australia, 4,272, Western Australia 2,512, and Tasmania 1,198

19 Much of the foregoing material comes from NSW Department of Education. *Progress in Education 1972* (Sydney, 1972)

20 Much of the material in this paragraph comes from *Commonwealth Year Book 1971*, Chapter 20

Chapter 3

1 See Pendred, G. E. 'Pre-School Centres in Australia' in *Review*

of Education in Australia 1955–62, ACER (Melbourne, 1964)
Chapter 10, and Bureau of Census and Statistics, *Official Year Book of the Commonwealth of Australia 1971*, 634

2   For an excellent demographic assessment of what lies ahead for Australian education, see Borrie, W. D. 'Resources Available for Education' in *Priorities in Australian Education*, Australian College of Education (Melbourne, 1972), 45–57

3   Much of the comment in this section is based on the latest review of secondary school facilities in Australia. See *Secondary Schooling in Australia*, Department of Education and Science (Canberra, 1972)

4   Among the universities which are thus experimenting are the Australian National University, Canberra, and the University of New England, Armidale

Chapter 4

1   Department of Education and Science & Australian Vice-Chancellors' Committee. *The 1961 Study* (Canberra, 1971), 28

2   *The 1961 Study*, 31

3   Springer, H. W. & Craig, T. (eds). *Commonwealth Universities Year Book* (1972)

4   Inevitably, this number is an underestimate since, increasingly, courses are being offered in semester and term units

5   Society for Research in Higher Education Ltd. *Higher Education Research in Australia and New Zealand* (1970), 22

6   Australian Vice-Chancellors' Committee. *Education Newsletter*, 1/71, 5

7   AV-CC. *Education Newsletter*, 2/71, 3–4

8   Australian Commission on Advanced Education. *Third Report* (Canberra, 1972), 2

9   *Third Report*, 8

10 Material on NSW colleges of advanced education provided by NSW Board of Advanced Education

11 Horne, B. & Wise, B. *Learning and Teaching in the CAEs 1969* (Melbourne, 1970), vol 1, 181–3

12 ACAE, *Third Report*, 53

13 *Third Report*, 54

Chapter 5

1   Borrie, W. D. 'Resources Available for Education', 45–57, in *Priorities in Australian Education*, Australian College of Education (Melbourne, 1972), 46

2 See Matthews, R. L. 'Finance for Education' in Arndt, H. W
   & Boxer, A. H. (eds), *The Australian Economy* (Melbourne, 1972),
   487–511, and *Commonwealth Year Book*, on which statistics in
   this section are largely based
3 For a fuller review of education in the ACT see recent issues of
   the *Commonwealth Year Book*
4 Australian Council for Educational Research. *38th Annual
   Report 1967–68* (Melbourne, 1969), 28
5 Ramsey, G. A. 'Curriculum Development in Secondary School
   Science', *Quarterly Review of Australian Education*, 5, no 2 (June
   1972), 9
6 Ramsey, 15
7 Department of Education and Science. *Commonwealth Programs
   in Education and Science* (Canberra, August 1971), 16

Chapter 6
1 Kandel, I. L. *Types of Administration* (Melbourne, 1961,
   reprint), 51
2 Kandel, 62
3 Cramer, J. F. & Browne, G. S. *Contemporary Education: A Comparative Study of National Systems* (New York, 1965, 2nd ed),
   389
4 Cramer & Browne, 389
5 Butts, R. Freeman. *Assumptions Underlying Australian Education*
   (Melbourne, 1955), 17
6 Ibid, 19
7 Ibid, 21–2
8 Ibid, see 75
9 Jackson, R. W. B. *Emergent Needs in Australian Education*
   (Toronto, 1961), 6
10 Jackson, 10–30
11 *Education News*, 3, no 2 (1951), 8; also Cramer & Browne, 389
12 Cramer & Browne, 390
13 Connell, W. F. *The Foundations of Secondary Education* (Melbourne 1962), 12
14 Connell, 17
15 Connell, 51–7
16 Karmel, P. H. 'Some Economic Aspects of Education', 24–48,
   in Cowan, R. W. T. (ed). *Education for Australians* (Melbourne,
   1964), 47
17 See Bassett, G. W. 'The Training of Teachers' and Walker, W. G.

'Educational Administration' in Cowan, *Education for Australians*, 142–61, 193–217

18 Hughes, P. 'The Government School', 85–90 in Walker, W. G. (ed). *School, College and University: The Administration of Education in Australia* (St Lucia, 1972), 88–9

19 Walker, *School, College and University*, xi

20 See *The Australian*, 29 July 1972

21 Schoenheimer, H. 'Bliss—But There Are Drawbacks in This Planned Utopia', *The Australian*, 4 August 1972

22 Thompson, L. H. S. *Looking Ahead in Education* (Melbourne, 1969)

23 Schoenheimer, H. P. 'Dollarships: and He Who Hath Gets More', *The Australian*, 19 July 1972

24 Ennor, H. reported in Victoria Institute of Colleges *VIC Newsletter*, 6, no 4 (September 1972), 8–13

25 Borrie, W. D. 'Resources Available for Education', 45–57, in *Priorities in Australian Education*, Australian College of Education (Melbourne, 1972)

26 *VIC Newsletter*, 6, no 4, 9

27 Partridge, P. H., quoted in *VIC Newsletter*, 6, no 4, 9

28 Fitzgerald, R. T. 'Emerging Issues in the Seventies', *Quarterly Review of Australian Education*, 5, no 3 (September 1972), 6–9

29 Election policies in this section are summarised from official party statements printed in *Education*, NSW Teachers' Federation, 22 November 1972, 276–7

30 *National Times*, 1–6 January 1973, 1, 7

Further Reading

Austin, A. G. *Australian Education 1788–1900* (Melbourne, 1961)

Australian Council for Educational Research. *Review of Education in Australia 1955–1962* (Melbourne, 1964). Reviews for previous years are also of interest

Barcan, Alan. *A Short History of Education in New South Wales* (Sydney, 1965)

Butts, R. Freeman. *Assumptions Underlying Australian Education* (Melbourne, 1955)

Cleverley, John F. *The First Generation: School and Society in Early Australia* (Sydney, 1971)

Cowan, R. W. T. (ed). *Education for Australians* (Melbourne, 1964)

Cramer, J. F. & Browne, G. S. *Contemporary Education: A Comparative Study of National Systems* (New York, 1965, 2nd ed)

Crawford, R. M. *Australia* (Sydney, 1960)

Davies, A. F. & Encel, S. *Australian Society* (Melbourne, 1965)

Department of Education and Science. *Education in Australia* (Canberra, 1970)

Department of Education and Science. *Secondary Schooling in Australia* (Canberra, 1972)

D'Urso, S. (ed). *Counterpoints: Critical Writings on Australian Education* (Sydney, 1971)

Fitzgerald, R. T. 'Emerging Issues in the Seventies', *Quarterly Review of Australian Education*, 5, no 3 (September 1972)

Gill, Peter (ed). *Catholic Education: Where is it Going?* (Melbourne, 1972)

Greenwood, Gordon (ed). *Australia: A Social and Political History* (Sydney, 1955)

Harman, G. S. & Selby Smith, C. (eds). *Australian Higher Education: Problems of a Developing System* (Sydney, 1972)

Horne, B. & Wise, B. *Learning and Teaching in the CAEs 1969*, 2 vols (Melbourne, 1970)

Horne, Donald. *The Lucky Country: Australia in the Sixties* (Harmondsworth, Middlesex, 1964)

Jones, Phillip E. *Comparative Education: Purpose and Method* (St Lucia, 1971), Chapter 1

Jones, Phillip E. 'The Present Pattern of Teacher Education' in Richardson, J. A. & Bowen, James (eds). *The Preparation of Teachers in Australia* (Melbourne, 1967), 54–68

McGregor, Craig. *Profile of Australia* (1966)

Maclaine, A. G. & Selby Smith, R. *Fundamental Issues in Australian Education* (Sydney, 1971)

McLaren, John. *Our Troubled Schools* (Melbourne, 1968)

Partridge, P. H. *Society, Schools and Progress in Australia* (Oxford, 1968)

Roper, Tom. *The Myth of Equality* (Melbourne, 1970)

Walker, W. G. (ed). *School, College and University: The Administration of Education in Australia* (St Lucia, 1972)

Ward, Russel. *The Australian Legend* (Melbourne, 1966, 2nd ed)

Whitelock, Derek A. *Adult Education in Australia* (Sydney, 1970)

Addendum

ELEVEN days after the formation of the Federal Labor government in late 1972, the new Prime Minister announced the establishment of an Interim Australian Schools Commission. Its specific aim was to formulate criteria for judging the allocation of future grants to non-government schools on the basis of need. Announcement of plans to establish, in a number of remote centres, special schools for aborigines in which the basic language of instruction was to be the local native dialect, with English being taught as a second language, followed. A major educational expansion programme for the Northern Territory was also being planned. The number of Commonwealth Teaching Scholarships, and allowances attached thereto, were substantially increased. The government foreshadowed help for isolated children, pre-schools and child-care training courses, and substantial assistance to the Australian film industry. Hints of further tertiary education expansion were given, aid for impoverished tertiary students was provided, and in March 1973 the Commonwealth government announced plans to abolish fees in all tertiary institutions from the beginning of 1974.

It was also announced that the AUC had been asked to investigate the establishment of an 'open' university, a Technical Education Commission was to inquire into the financing of technical and trade education, further funds were to be made available for libraries in CAEs, a national dental health plan for schools would be started, a National Advisory Committee on the Handicapped was foreshadowed and the Commonwealth was to

K 145

investigate the need for pre-school and child-care centres and to foster research in these fields.

In May 1973, the government decided to establish an Education Research Institute as well as to inquire into the arts and provide more funds for them. At about the same time, the first recommendations of the Interim Australian Schools Commission (quickly becoming known as the Karmel Report) were accepted: these provided for adjusting Commonwealth grants to non-government schools according to categories based on teacher/ pupil ratios. Thus, Cabinet agreed to a total of 105 schools receiving almost no aid after 1973, but to many other less favoured categories receiving more. In the media there was severe criticism of this decision, including some Catholic opposition. Meanwhile, states and teacher organisations continued to seek more aid for school-building and for employing more teachers in state educational systems. Other matters claiming the new government's attention included a recommendation for spending about $207m on teacher education over 30 months (accepted in the main), a concern about establishing community recreation centres, and a favourable decision about new senior (ie matriculation) colleges for the Australian Capital Territory.

In August 1973, the first budget of the new government provided for a 92 per cent increase in expenditure on education. Actual Commonwealth expenditure in 1972/3 had been $439m and the expenditure proposed for 1973/4 was $843m. Education therefore constituted the fastest growing component of the budget.

In his budget speech the Treasurer said that the assumption of full financial responsibility for tertiary education at universities, colleges of advanced education, state teachers' colleges and other approved teachers' colleges, including the abolition of fees at all these institutions and technical colleges, would entail an additional outlay of $179m in 1973/4. He also announced, inter alia, that from the beginning of 1974, non-competitive means-tested living allowances would be offered to all full-time unbonded

Australian students admitted to approved courses in tertiary and approved post-secondary institutions. To assist low-income families to educate their children in the final two years of secondary school, means-tested educational allowances of up to $304 per annum would also be paid from the beginning of 1974.

(Sources: *Hansard, The Australian, Sydney Morning Herald*)

	1972/3 Actual	$ million 1973/4 Estimate	Increase on 1972/3
Universities	189·8	312·8	+ 123·0
CAEs and teachers' colleges	72·0	183·5	+ 111·5
Technical education	19·2	45·9	+ 26·8
Schools and pre-schools	124·1	245·4	+ 121·3
Special groups (including aboriginal and migrant education)	25·5	45·0	+ 19·5
Administrative and other expenditure	9·3	11·3	+ 1·9
Less recoveries	0·7	0·6	− 0·1
Total Education	439·3	843·4	+ 404·1

Acknowledgements

GRATEFUL acknowledgement is expressed to the following for permission to quote or use copyright material: The Commonwealth Bureau of Census and Statistics and Department of Education, Canberra (for table on 'Grades in Australian Schools, 1972'); the Director-General of Education, Department of Education, New South Wales (for the map of education directorates); Harcourt Brace Jovanovich, Inc. and the authors, J. A. Cramer and G. S. Browne (for permission to quote from *Contemporary Education: A Comparative Study of National Systems* [2nd ed]); Hutchinson Publishing Group Ltd and the author, R. M. Crawford (for permission to quote from *Australia*); Oxford University Press (Australia) and Russel Ward (for permission to quote from *The Australian Legend*), and the University of Queensland Press and the editor, Professor W. G. Walker (for permission to quote from *School, College and University: The Administration of Education in Australia*).

Finally, I would like to thank a number of my students at the University of New England for valuable assistance in the collection of material in the early stages of preparation.

P. E. J.

Index

Bold type indicates a map or figure